FINANCIAL FOUNDATIONS OF CERAMICS

COSTING, PRICING, AND PROFITABILITY

DR. GHANSHYAM TRIVEDI

Made with ♥ on the Notion Press Platform
www.notionpress.com

"Dedicated to the artisans whose hands mold beauty from clay, the entrepreneurs whose vision shapes the industry's future, and the enthusiasts whose passion fuels its timeless allure. May this book serve as a beacon, guiding you towards prosperity and sustainability in the world of ceramics."

ᐅᐅᐅ

Contents

Contents

Prayer

गुरुर्ब्रह्मा गुरुर्विष्णु
गुरुर्देवो महेश्वरा

गुरुर्साक्षात परब्रह्म
तस्मै श्री गुरवे नमः

About The Author

Ghanshyam Trivedi, born on September 18, 1946, in India, stands as a luminary in the ceramic industry with a career spanning over four decades. Armed with an MSc and an LL.B., Mr. Trivedi has not only contributed to the scientific and legal realms but has also played a pivotal role in transforming the landscape of the ceramic tile sector both nationally and internationally.

A true visionary, Ghanshyam has been at the forefront of innovation, sustainability, and leadership in the ceramic industry. As a testament to his dedication and expertise, he has held prestigious positions such as the President of the Kadi Industrial Association and the All India Pottery Manufacturers Association, showcasing his influence and commitment to the sector. His tenure as a council member of the Indian Ceramic Society further highlights his dedication to advancing ceramic science and education.

Beyond his leadership roles, Mr. Trivedi has significantly contributed to the advancement of ceramic manufacturing techniques, leading to more sustainable and innovative practices. His roles as Director at several leading companies, including Somany Ceramics Ltd and Vidres India Ceramics Pvt Ltd, underline his strategic prowess and operational expertise.

Ghanshyam's academic contributions are equally noteworthy, with publications in esteemed journals and presentations at international conferences. These works not only reflect his deep understanding of ceramic science but also his ability to navigate the complexities of green manufacturing and global market trends.

His commitment to education and skill development is evident through his involvement in various advisory and executive committees, including the Central Glass and Research Institute and the Gujarat Power Engineering and Research Institute. Furthermore, his international exposure, marked by a study tour with the Rotary International Group Study Exchange Team to Canada and the USA, has enriched his perspective on global manufacturing practices and innovations.

<u>PROFESSIONAL QUALIFICATIONS/MEMBERSHIPS</u>

Associate Member of the Institute of Cost Accountants of India

Member, All India Management Association.

Member, All India Pottery Manufactures' Association

Member, Indian Ceramic Society

Ex-Member, American Ceramic Society.

<u>POSITIONS HELD</u>

President, Kadi Industrial Association, Kadi.

Twice, President, All India Pottery Manufacturers Association

Twice Council Member- Indian Ceramic Society.

Member Advisory Committee of the Central Glass and Research Institute, Naroda, Ahmedabad.

Committee Member -Gujarat Power Engineering and Research Institute, Mehsana.

For One Year, Visiting Faculty of the Sahajanand Multicourse College, Ahmedabad.

The Chairman,76th Annual Session of the Indian Ceramic Society, Ahmedabad.

Ex-committee member of the ceramic raw materials and ceramic tiles committee of the BIS (CHD-9, CED-3, CED-5)

Ex-Member of Board of Management, P.S. Science & H.D. Patel Arts College, Kadi

Executive Committee member- Gujarat Chamber of Commerce (2008-09)

Member-Rotary International Group Study Exchange Team, study tour of Canada-USA

PUBLICATIONS/PAPERS

"Costing in the Starch Industry" – The Management Accountant

"Ceramic Glazed Tiles – Prospects and Problems". (Wheel)

"Green Manufacturing Initiatives in Ceramic Tiles Manufacturing"- Papers read at The Materials Science & Technology -2014- Pittsburgh

"Increase in Vitrified Tile Production by the Use of Borate Flux"- Conference Qualicer-2014-Spain

"Simple and fast method to measure Spray dried Granule Size Distribution" – Papers Read at the International Conference on Emergence of New Era in Glass and Ceramics- NEGC2013- AHMEDABAD

ASSOCIATION WITH CORPORATES

(1) Director, Somany Ceramics Ltd

(2) Director, Somany Bathwares Ltd

(3) Director, Yogi Cerachem Pvt Ltd

(4) Director, Vidres India Ceramic Pvt Ltd

(5) Director, Trans India Ceramic Pvt Ltd

(6) Director, Xphere India Foundation

(7) Director, Eurofrits India Pvt Ltd

(8) Director, Earthluxe Mineral LLP

(9) Member, The Board Of Management – Saraspur Nagrik Co.Operative Bank Ltd; Ahmedabad

(10) Advisor, Central Glass and Research Institute, Naroda, Ahmedabad.

(11) Life Member, Indian Ceramic Society

(12) Life Member, All India Pottery Manufacturers Association

(13) President, Kadi Industrial Association, Kadi.

(14) President, All India Pottery Manufacturers Association (2022 – 2024)

(15) Associate Member of the Institute of Cost Accountants of India

(16) Member, All India Management Association.

(17) Member, American Ceramic Society. (till 2017)

(18) Member (Committee) -Gujarat Power Engineering and Research Institute, Mehsana.

(19) Member of Board of Management, P.S. Science & H.D. Patel Arts College, Kadi

(20) Executive Committee member- Gujarat Chamber of Commerce (2008-09)

(21) Member-Rotary international Group Study Exchange Team, study tour of Canada-USA (1975-76)

(22) Ex-committee member of the ceramic raw materials and ceramic tiles committee of the BIS (CHD-9, CED-3, CED-5)

(23) The Chairman,76th Annual Session of the Indian Ceramic Society, Ahmedabad.

(24) For One Year, Visiting Faculty of the Sahajanand Multicourse College, Ahmedabad.

(25) Twice, Council Member- Indian Ceramic Society.

(26) CEO/Executive Director at Somany Ceramics Ltd (1987 – 2019)

The above encapsulates the essence of Ghanshyam Trivedi's remarkable journey from a dedicated student of science and law to a pioneering figure in the ceramic industry. His legacy is not just in the tiles and ceramics that bear his mark but in the sustainable practices, innovative technologies, and global collaborations he championed. Through his work, Mr. Trivedi has not only shaped the present of the ceramic industry but also laid a solid foundation for its future.

❦❦❦

Preface

In the labyrinth of global commerce, the ceramics industry emerges as a testament to the blend of ancient craft and modern economics. "Financial Foundations of Ceramics: Costing, Pricing, and Profitability" seeks to illuminate the path for entrepreneurs, artisans, and business managers navigating the intricate financial landscapes of this timeless trade. This book is a compass, designed to guide you through the complexities of financial management in the ceramics sector, from the crafting table to the global market.

Ceramics, with their rich history and cultural significance, are more than mere objects of utility or beauty; they are vessels of tradition and innovation. However, the journey from clay to cherished object is fraught with financial challenges and opportunities. Understanding the cost structures, pricing strategies, and paths to profitability in this field is crucial for any business aiming to thrive. This preface aims to set the stage for a deep dive into the financial underpinnings that support and sustain the ceramics industry.

The inspiration for this work stems from a recognition of the gap between the artistic mastery of ceramics and the financial acumen required to ensure their creators' sustainability and success. Many ceramicists embark on their journey with a passion for the art, only to find themselves navigating the treacherous waters of business finance with little guidance. This book aims to bridge that gap, offering clear, concise, and practical advice on managing the financial aspects of a ceramics business.

Each chapter of this book is carefully crafted to address the critical financial elements of the ceramics industry. We begin by exploring the fundamentals of costing, breaking down the components that contribute to the cost of producing ceramics, from raw materials to labor and overheads. Understanding these elements is the first step toward achieving financial sustainability, enabling artists and entrepreneurs to make informed decisions about production and pricing.

Pricing strategies are another cornerstone of financial success in the ceramics industry. This book delves into various pricing models, guiding readers on how to set prices that reflect the value of their work while remaining competitive in the market. We explore the psychological aspects of pricing, the impact of market demand, and strategies for premium pricing of artisanal pieces.

Profitability, the ultimate goal for any business, is examined through multiple lenses. We discuss how to analyze financial performance, manage cash flows, and reinvest profits to fuel growth. The book addresses common financial pitfalls in the ceramics industry and provides strategies for overcoming them, including diversification of product lines and markets, and leveraging technology to improve efficiency and reach.

In addition to the core topics of costing, pricing, and profitability, this book touches on the broader financial ecosystem of the ceramics industry. We explore financing options available to ceramicists, from traditional loans to crowdfunding and grants specifically targeted at artists. International trade and finance, a critical aspect for those looking to expand beyond local markets, is also covered, providing insights into navigating the complexities of exporting and importing, currency exchange, and international payments.

The narrative is enriched with case studies and real-life examples, drawing on the experiences of ceramic artists and businesses from around the world. These stories bring to life the financial principles discussed, showcasing the diverse ways in which ceramicists have tackled financial challenges and harnessed opportunities to thrive.

This book also acknowledges the evolving landscape of the ceramics industry, shaped by technological advancements, changing consumer preferences, and global economic trends. We discuss the impact of online marketplaces, social media, and digital marketing on the economics of ceramics, offering guidance on how to leverage these tools for financial gain.

As we navigate through the chapters, the emphasis remains on practicality and applicability. The goal is not only to impart knowledge but to empower readers to apply these financial principles in their own businesses. Worksheets, templates, and checklists are provided throughout the book, enabling readers to engage with the content actively and personalize the insights to their own contexts.

"Financial Foundations of Ceramics: Costing, Pricing, and Profitability" is more than a manual; it is a companion for anyone in the ceramics industry seeking to build a financially sustainable business. Whether you are a seasoned ceramicist looking to refine your business model, an entrepreneur venturing into the world of ceramics, or a student aspiring to merge artistic passion with business acumen, this book is for you.

In writing this book, my hope is to demystify the financial aspects of running a ceramics business, making them accessible and actionable. The journey of each ceramic piece, from clay to completion, is a story of transformation. Similarly, the journey of financial mastery is one of empowerment, enabling artists and business owners to secure the future of their craft and their livelihoods.

As you turn the pages, I invite you to approach the content with an open mind and a willingness to explore new perspectives on the financial management of your ceramics business. The principles and strategies outlined here are the culmination of extensive research, interviews with industry experts, and my own experiences in the world of ceramics and finance.

Let this book be the kiln in which your financial acumen is fired and strengthened, ready to withstand the pressures of the business world and emerge successful. Welcome to the financial foundations of ceramics, where art meets economics in the pursuit of profitability and passion.

Dr. Ghanshyam Trivedi
Ahmedabad, Gujrat, India

ᐅᐅᐅ

ONE

Introduction to the Ceramics Industry

Overview of the ceramics sector, its economic significance, and the unique financial challenges it faces.

The ceramics industry, with its rich heritage and innovative future, stands as a significant contributor to the global economy. This sector, which encompasses a wide range of products from household pottery and decorative items to industrial and high-tech ceramic applications, embodies a fusion of art, tradition, and technology. Despite its age-old roots, the industry continues to evolve, facing both timeless challenges and new financial hurdles.

Historical Context and Modern Evolution

The journey of ceramics from ancient craftsmanship to modern industry is a testament to human ingenuity. Early civilizations recognized the utility of fired clay for creating durable, functional items, and over millennia, this evolved into both an art form and a critical component of industrial applications. Today, ceramics are not only central to cultural expressions but also to advancements in sectors such as healthcare, electronics, and aerospace, thanks to the material's unique properties like heat resistance, durability, and electrical insulation.

Economic Significance

The economic impact of the ceramics industry is multifaceted, contributing billions of dollars to global GDP. Its significance is not just in the value of the goods produced but also in the employment it provides across the supply chain—from raw material extraction and processing to manufacturing, distribution, and retail. In regions rich in ceramic heritage, such as Jingdezhen in China, Faenza in Italy, and Arita in Japan, the industry is a cornerstone of local economies, supporting tourism and cultural preservation.

Moreover, the sector's innovation-driven areas, particularly advanced ceramics, are pivotal in strategic industries, fostering national competitiveness and technological advancement. The economic ripple effects are substantial, influencing sectors like energy, defense, and telecommunications.

The Craft and Business of Ceramics

At the heart of the ceramics industry lie the dual aspects of craft and commerce. For many artisans and small businesses, ceramics is not just a means of livelihood but also an expression of creativity. This blend poses unique financial challenges, as the cost structures and market dynamics can be significantly different from those of mass-produced goods. Artisans must navigate the intricacies of raw material costs, studio rent, equipment maintenance, and labor, all while competing in a market that increasingly values uniqueness and craftsmanship.

Unique Financial Challenges

The financial landscape of the ceramics industry is characterized by several unique challenges:

High Initial Investment: Setting up a ceramics studio or manufacturing facility requires significant upfront investment in equipment such as kilns, pottery wheels, and mold-making tools, as well as in securing a suitable workspace.

Variable Raw Material Costs: The prices of clay, glazes, and other raw materials can fluctuate based on availability, quality, and geopolitical factors, impacting production costs and profit margins.

Energy Intensity: Ceramics production is energy-intensive, especially the firing process, leading to high utility costs that can erode profitability, particularly in regions with higher energy prices.

Market Competition: The industry faces competition from low-cost mass production, especially from countries with lower labor and production costs, challenging artisans and smaller producers to differentiate their products through quality, design, and storytelling.

Technological Investment: Keeping pace with advancements in production techniques and materials science requires ongoing investment in technology and training, a significant hurdle for smaller operators.

Environmental Regulations: Compliance with increasingly stringent environmental regulations related to emissions and waste management can entail additional costs, particularly for older facilities needing upgrades.

Navigating the Financial Landscape

To thrive in this complex financial environment, ceramics businesses must adopt strategic approaches to cost management, pricing, and market positioning. This includes leveraging technology for efficiency gains, exploring sustainable practices that can also reduce costs, and developing strong brand identities to command premium prices. Additionally, tapping into emerging markets and applications for ceramics, from 3D printing to biomedical implants, offers pathways to diversification and growth.

The Role of Innovation and Sustainability

Innovation in materials, processes, and business models is crucial for addressing the financial challenges of the ceramics industry. Advances in materials science, such as the development of tougher, more versatile ceramics, expand the range of applications and markets. Process innovations, including energy-efficient kilns and waste recycling, can significantly reduce production costs and environmental impact. Moreover, business model innovations, like direct-to-consumer sales channels and experiential marketing, can enhance profitability in a competitive landscape.

Sustainability has emerged as both a challenge and an opportunity. As consumers and regulators increasingly prioritize environmental impact, ceramics businesses that adopt sustainable practices not only reduce their costs and risks but also enhance their brand value and market appeal.

The ceramics industry, straddling the worlds of art, tradition, and cutting-edge technology, occupies a unique place in the global economy. Its contributions are measured not only in economic terms but also in cultural richness and technological progress. However, navigating the financial intricacies of this sector requires a deep understanding of its challenges and opportunities. As the industry continues to evolve, balancing tradition with innovation and embracing sustainability will be paramount for its long-term success. By integrating sustainable financial practices, leveraging technology, and adapting to changing consumer preferences, ceramics businesses can thrive in an increasingly competitive market landscape.

ϷϷϷ

Summary

The ceramics industry, a blend of ancient artistry and modern commerce, holds a significant place in the global economy. This sector encompasses a wide range of products, from household pottery and decorative items to industrial and high-tech ceramic components. Its economic importance is not only rooted in its contribution to global trade but also in its role in cultural heritage and innovation. Despite its rich history and economic value, the ceramics industry faces unique financial challenges. These include the high costs of raw materials and energy, the need for significant upfront investments in equipment and technology, and the intricacies of managing cash flow in a market where the production process can be lengthy and the demand fluctuates. Additionally, artisans and businesses must navigate the complexities of pricing their creations in a way that reflects both their artistic value and production costs, while also remaining competitive in a diverse and ever-changing market. Understanding these financial hurdles is crucial for anyone looking to succeed in the ceramics sector.

ᐅᐅᐅ

TWO

Basic Financial Principles for Ceramics Businesses

Fundamentals of finance, including cash flow, profit margins, and balance sheets, tailored for the ceramics industry.

The ceramics industry, embodying a blend of artistry and commerce, stands as a testament to the enduring allure and utility of ceramic goods. From intricate pottery and sculptures to industrial components and building materials, ceramics encompass a vast range of products pivotal to both everyday life and numerous sectors of the global economy. As we delve into the basic financial principles for ceramics businesses, it becomes essential to tailor these fundamentals to the unique characteristics and challenges of the ceramics sector. This chapter aims to equip ceramic artists, entrepreneurs, and managers with the financial acumen required to navigate the industry's complexities, focusing on cash flow, profit margins, and balance sheets.

Understanding Cash Flow in the Ceramics Industry

Cash flow, the lifeblood of any business, represents the net amount of cash being transferred into and out of a business over a specific period. For ceramics businesses, managing cash flow is particularly challenging due to the cyclical nature of sales, which may be influenced by seasonal trends, consumer demand fluctuations, and the time-intensive processes involved in ceramics production. Effective cash flow management entails meticulous planning of inventory purchases, careful timing of sales efforts, and judicious management of receivables and payables. Ceramics businesses must adopt robust forecasting tools to anticipate cash flow needs, ensuring that they have sufficient liquidity to cover operational expenses, invest in new projects, and navigate through lean periods.

The Importance of Profit Margins

Profit margins, indicating the percentage of revenue that remains after accounting for the cost of goods sold (COGS), are crucial for assessing the financial health of a ceramics business. The ceramics industry faces unique cost considerations, such as the high costs of raw materials (clay, glazes, etc.), energy (for firing kilns), and labor (especially for handcrafted items). To maintain healthy profit margins, ceramics businesses must not only manage these costs effectively but also develop pricing strategies that reflect the value of their products. This involves understanding the market, the uniqueness and quality of the products offered, and the target customer base. Strategies such as value-based pricing can be particularly effective in the ceramics industry, where the aesthetic and functional value of products plays a significant role in consumer purchasing decisions.

Mastering the Balance Sheet

The balance sheet provides a snapshot of a company's financial condition at a specific point in time, detailing assets, liabilities, and shareholders' equity. For ceramics businesses, the balance sheet is an essential tool for assessing the value of inventory (an important asset), understanding debt levels (liabilities), and evaluating the overall equity position of the business. Given the potentially high inventory levels in the ceramics industry, due to the need to stock a diverse range of products and the time required to produce them, managing inventory valuation is critical. This involves regularly assessing the market value of inventory, adjusting for any obsolescence or damage, and ensuring that inventory levels are optimized – neither too high, causing unnecessary capital tie-up and storage costs, nor too low, risking stockouts and lost sales.

Navigating the Financial Landscape of Ceramics

To navigate the financial landscape of the ceramics industry successfully, businesses must also be adept at interpreting financial ratios derived from cash flow statements, income statements, and balance sheets. Ratios such as the current ratio (liquidity measurement), debt-to-equity ratio (leverage measurement), and gross margin ratio (profitability measurement) provide invaluable insights into the financial health and operational efficiency of a ceramics business. Furthermore, understanding the cost structure of ceramics production is vital. This includes direct costs like materials and labor, as well as indirect costs such as utilities, rent, and equipment depreciation. By closely monitoring these costs, ceramics businesses can identify opportunities for cost savings, efficiency improvements, and ultimately, profit maximization.

Leveraging Financial Insights for Strategic Decision-Making

The integration of financial management into strategic decision-making is essential for the growth and sustainability of ceramics businesses. This involves using financial data to inform decisions on product development, market expansion, investment in new technologies or processes, and other strategic initiatives. For example, analysis of profit margins by product line can reveal which items are most profitable and should be the focus of marketing efforts. Similarly, cash flow forecasts can help determine the feasibility of expanding production capacity or entering new markets.

In conclusion, mastering the basic financial principles of cash flow, profit margins, and balance sheets, while navigating the unique challenges of the ceramics industry, is crucial for the success of ceramics businesses. By developing a deep understanding of these financial fundamentals and applying them with a keen awareness of the industry's specificities, ceramics entrepreneurs and managers can build resilient, profitable businesses that thrive in the dynamic global marketplace. As the ceramics industry continues to evolve, driven by technological advancements, changing consumer preferences, and global economic trends, a solid foundation in financial management will remain an indispensable asset for those seeking to explore the artistic and commercial potential of ceramics.

ϸϸϸ

Summary

In the ceramics industry, mastering basic financial principles is essential for sustaining and growing a business. This includes a deep understanding of cash flow, profit margins, and balance sheets, all tailored to the unique context of ceramics. Cash flow, the lifeblood of any business, is crucial in an industry where the production cycle can be prolonged, necessitating careful planning to ensure that incoming revenues can cover ongoing expenses. Profit margins in the ceramics sector are influenced by factors such as the cost of materials, labor, and the intricacies of the production process, requiring a strategic approach to pricing products competitively while still ensuring profitability. Additionally, maintaining a healthy balance sheet by managing assets, liabilities, and equity is vital for long-term financial stability and attracting potential investors or loans. These financial fundamentals, when applied thoughtfully, empower ceramics businesses to navigate the economic challenges of the industry, from fluctuating market demands to the high costs associated with craftsmanship and materials.

ᗊᗊᗊ

THREE

Cost Structures in Ceramics Production

—◦♭◦—

Detailed analysis of fixed and variable costs in ceramics, from materials to labor and overhead.

Understanding the cost structures in ceramics production is pivotal for anyone operating within this field. The ceramics industry, known for its blend of artistry and technicality, encompasses a wide array of processes and products, from handcrafted pottery and sculptures to industrial ceramics and tiles. Each of these products comes with its own set of financial challenges, primarily revolving around the costs of production. This chapter delves deep into the fixed and variable costs associated with ceramics production, providing a comprehensive analysis aimed at equipping ceramics entrepreneurs with the knowledge to optimize their production costs and enhance profitability.

Fixed Costs in Ceramics Production

Fixed costs are expenses that do not change with the volume of production. These costs are incurred regardless of whether the ceramics studio or factory is producing at full capacity, a reduced volume, or not at all. Understanding these costs is crucial for budgeting and financial planning.

Studio or Factory Rent: One of the most significant fixed costs, the rent for the space where ceramics are produced remains constant, regardless of production volume. Choosing the right location can significantly impact this cost, with studios in urban areas typically commanding higher rents than those in more rural settings.

Equipment Purchase and Depreciation: Equipment such as kilns, wheel throwers, and mixers represent substantial investments. While the initial purchase is a one-time expense, the depreciation of this equipment over its useful life is considered a fixed cost. Regular maintenance is also necessary to extend the life of the equipment, incurring additional fixed expenses.

Insurance: Insurance costs, including property, liability, and workers' compensation insurance, are fixed costs that protect the business from unforeseen events. These costs vary depending on the coverage amounts and the specific risks associated with the ceramics production environment.

Salaries of Permanent Staff: Salaries for full-time employees, including studio managers, designers, and administrative staff, are fixed costs. These expenses remain constant regardless of production levels, emphasizing the importance of efficient staff utilization.

Variable Costs in Ceramics Production

Unlike fixed costs, variable costs fluctuate with the level of production. Managing these costs effectively is key to maintaining profitability, especially during periods of fluctuating demand.

Raw Materials: The cost of clay, glazes, and other materials directly correlates with the volume of production. Efficient inventory management and purchasing strategies can help minimize these costs, such as buying in bulk or negotiating favorable terms with suppliers.

Labor: While salaries for permanent staff are fixed, labor costs for hourly or piece-rate workers vary with production volume. Managing labor costs requires balancing the need for skilled craftsmanship with production demands, ensuring that labor efficiency is maximized.

Utilities: The consumption of gas, electricity, and water, particularly for running kilns, varies significantly with production levels. Energy-efficient practices and equipment can help reduce these variable costs.

Packaging and Shipping: As the volume of products shipped to customers increases, so do the costs for packaging materials and freight. Optimizing packaging design for cost-efficiency and negotiating favorable shipping rates can mitigate these variable expenses.

Overhead Costs in Ceramics Production

Overhead costs, while somewhat fixed, include a variety of expenses that support the production process but are not directly tied to any specific product.

Administrative Expenses: These include office supplies, software subscriptions for design and business management, and administrative salaries. Efficient administration is crucial for minimizing these overhead costs.

Marketing and Sales: Costs associated with promoting the ceramics business, from digital marketing to attending trade shows, are considered overhead. These expenses can vary but are essential for generating demand and expanding the customer base.

Research and Development (R&D): Investing in R&D is vital for innovation and staying competitive in the ceramics industry. These costs can include experimenting with new materials, techniques, and product designs.

Analyzing Cost Structures for Profitability

Understanding the nuances of fixed, variable, and overhead costs is just the beginning. Ceramics businesses must analyze these costs in relation to their production volumes and sales prices to ensure profitability. This involves:

Break-even Analysis: Determining the production volume at which total revenues equal total costs, highlighting the minimum sales required to cover all expenses.

Cost-Volume-Profit (CVP) Analysis: Understanding how changes in production volumes, costs, and prices affect profitability, enabling strategic decision-making regarding pricing, production levels, and cost management.

Margin Analysis: Evaluating the profit margins of different products to prioritize those with the highest return on investment and adjust the product mix accordingly.

Strategic Cost Management in Ceramics Production

Achieving a competitive edge in the ceramics industry requires more than just minimizing costs; it demands strategic cost management. This includes:

Investing in Technology: Leveraging automation and energy-efficient kilns can significantly reduce labor and utility costs.

Supply Chain Optimization: Developing strong relationships with suppliers and exploring alternative material sources can lower raw material costs.

Product Lifecycle Management: Continually assessing the profitability of each product line and making adjustments to the product mix based on market demand and cost structures.

The financial health of a ceramics business heavily relies on the ability to manage and optimize its cost structures. By understanding and strategically managing fixed, variable, and overhead costs, ceramics entrepreneurs can make informed decisions that enhance efficiency, reduce waste, and improve profitability. This chapter provides the foundational knowledge required to navigate the complex financial landscape of ceramics production, setting the stage for successful business operations in this creatively rich and economically significant industry.

Summary

The production of ceramics involves a complex interplay of fixed and variable costs that significantly influence the overall cost structure of businesses within this industry. Fixed costs, such as the purchase of kilns and other essential equipment, represent investments that do not change with the volume of production. These costs provide the foundation for a ceramics business, requiring strategic planning and management to ensure profitability over time. On the other hand, variable costs fluctuate with production levels and include raw materials, such as clay and glazes, as well as labor costs directly associated with the crafting and firing processes. Overhead costs, encompassing everything from studio rent to utilities and marketing expenses, also play a critical role in the ceramics production cost structure. A detailed analysis of these cost components is essential for ceramics businesses to develop effective pricing strategies, manage budgets efficiently, and ultimately achieve a sustainable financial model in the competitive landscape of the ceramics industry.

ᐯᐯᐯ

FOUR

CALCULATING PRODUCTION COSTS

Step-by-step guide to accurately calculating costs associated with ceramics production, including case studies.

Calculating production costs with precision is crucial for the success of any ceramics business, whether it's a small studio crafting handmade pottery or a larger company producing ceramic tiles on a mass scale. This chapter aims to demystify the process of determining production costs in the ceramics industry, providing a clear, step-by-step guide that encompasses all factors from raw materials to finished goods. By incorporating real-life case studies, we illuminate the practical application of these principles, offering insights into how accurate cost calculation can lead to more informed pricing, better financial planning, and ultimately, increased profitability.

Step 1: Identifying Direct Materials Costs

The first step in calculating production costs is to quantify the costs of the direct materials used. For ceramics, this includes clay, glazes, and other decorative elements. It's essential to track the quantity of materials used per batch or item to determine the cost accurately.

Case Study: Pottery Studio

A small pottery studio measures the amount of clay and glaze used for a series of mugs. By calculating the cost per pound of clay and per ounce of glaze, they determine the direct materials cost for each mug.

Step 2: Calculating Direct Labor Costs

Direct labor costs encompass the wages of employees who are directly involved in creating the ceramic pieces. This calculation should account for the time spent on each piece or batch, from preparation through to the final touches.

Case Study: Ceramic Sculpture Workshop

In a workshop specializing in ceramic sculptures, the direct labor cost is calculated by tracking the hours spent by artists on each sculpture. By multiplying the hours by the wage rate, the workshop can allocate a precise labor cost to each piece.

Step 3: Assessing Manufacturing Overhead

Manufacturing overhead includes all the production costs not directly tied to a specific product but necessary for the manufacturing process. This includes the costs of utilities for firing kilns, equipment depreciation, and maintenance.

Case Study: Industrial Ceramics Manufacturer

An industrial manufacturer of ceramic components allocates

overhead costs by determining the kiln's operational costs per hour, including energy consumption and maintenance. These costs are then spread over the products based on kiln usage time.

Step 4: Determining Total Production Costs

The total production cost is the sum of direct materials, direct labor, and manufacturing overhead. This figure provides a comprehensive view of what it costs to produce each item or batch of ceramics.

Case Study: Handmade Tile Maker

A company producing handmade ceramic tiles calculates the total production cost by adding the materials, labor, and a portion of overhead costs associated with each batch of tiles. This helps in setting prices that cover costs and yield a profit.

Step 5: Calculating Cost Per Unit

To find the cost per unit, divide the total production costs by the number of units produced. This figure is critical for pricing decisions, ensuring each sale covers the cost and contributes to profitability.

Case Study: Decorative Ceramics Studio

The studio calculates the cost per unit for a batch of decorative vases by dividing the total production cost of the batch by the number of vases produced. This cost per unit guides their pricing strategy.

Case Studies in Depth

Pottery Studio Case Study: Streamlining Materials Usage

The pottery studio from our first case study discovered through careful tracking that standardizing mug sizes could reduce clay and glaze waste. By negotiating better prices for bulk purchases of materials and refining their production techniques, they were able to decrease the direct materials cost per mug, improving their overall profit margins.

Ceramic Sculpture Workshop Case Study: Labor Efficiency

The sculpture workshop implemented time-tracking software to more accurately assess the time spent on each piece. By identifying and training on techniques that could reduce labor time without compromising quality, the workshop increased its production capacity and reduced the direct labor cost per sculpture, thereby enhancing profitability.

Industrial Ceramics Manufacturer Case Study: Overhead Reduction

The industrial ceramics manufacturer invested in more energy-efficient kilns and implemented a scheduled maintenance program to reduce downtime and repair costs. These measures lowered the manufacturing overhead, decreasing the cost allocated to each component and increasing competitive pricing capabilities.

Handmade Tile Maker Case Study: Overhead Allocation

By analyzing their production process, the handmade tile maker realized that certain designs required significantly more kiln time, contributing to higher overhead costs. They adjusted their pricing model to reflect the varying overhead costs associated with different tile designs, ensuring each product line was priced appropriately for profitability.

Accurately calculating production costs is a fundamental aspect of financial management in the ceramics industry. By meticulously tracking direct materials, labor, and overhead costs, businesses can gain a clear understanding of the expenses involved in their production processes. This detailed cost knowledge enables more informed pricing strategies, aids in financial planning, and supports strategic decision-making aimed at enhancing efficiency and profitability.

The case studies presented in this chapter highlight how practical applications of these cost calculation principles can lead to tangible improvements in a business's financial health. By embracing these methodologies, ceramics businesses can better navigate the complexities of production cost management, setting a solid foundation for sustained success in the competitive world of ceramics.

ᐯᐯᐯ

Summary

"Calculating Production Costs" provides a practical, step-by-step guide tailored for ceramics businesses aiming to accurately determine the costs associated with their production processes. This essential resource breaks down the methodology for calculating both direct and indirect costs, including raw materials, labor, overheads, and equipment depreciation. The guide emphasizes the importance of accounting for every element involved in the creation of ceramics, from initial clay purchase to the final firing. Incorporating real-world case studies, it illustrates how different ceramics businesses apply these principles to their operations, offering insights into the challenges and solutions encountered. By detailing this approach, the guide empowers ceramics entrepreneurs to achieve a clear understanding of their production costs, laying the foundation for strategic pricing, budgeting, and financial planning that ensures the viability and growth of their businesses in the competitive market.

ᐅᐅᐅ

FIVE

PRICING STRATEGIES FOR CERAMICS PRODUCTS

Examination of various pricing models (cost-plus, value-based, competition-based) and their applicability to ceramics.

The art of pricing ceramics transcends mere arithmetic; it embodies a nuanced understanding of the market, the inherent value of the craftsmanship, and the competitive landscape. In the ceramics industry, where products range from functional ware to exquisite art pieces, determining the right price point is pivotal.

Here we will discuss various pricing strategies, including cost-plus, value-based, and competition-based models, examining their applicability and effectiveness within the diverse realms of ceramics.

Cost-Plus Pricing Strategy

The cost-plus model is a straightforward approach where a fixed percentage is added to the production cost to determine the selling price. This method ensures all costs are covered and a profit margin is secured. However, its simplicity can also be a limitation, as it does not consider market demand or perceived value.

Application in Ceramics: Ideal for studios producing functional ceramics in relatively standard designs, where production costs are predictable, and market prices are stable. This method ensures profitability but may not capture the full value of more artistic or unique pieces.

Case Study: A pottery studio producing handcrafted mugs calculates the cost of materials, labor, and overhead for each mug to be $15. Applying a 50% markup, the selling price is set at $22.50. This straightforward approach covers costs and secures a consistent profit margin, suitable for their functional product line.

Value-Based Pricing Strategy

Value-based pricing centers on the perceived value of the product to the customer rather than the cost of production. This strategy can capture premiums for craftsmanship, brand reputation, and the artistic value of ceramics, potentially leading to higher profit margins.

Application in Ceramics: Particularly effective for unique, artistically significant pieces or those by well-known artists. It requires an understanding of the target market and the value customers place on the uniqueness, aesthetic appeal, and craftsmanship of the ceramics.

Case Study: An acclaimed ceramic artist whose work is recognized for its unique style and artistic merit prices her sculptures based on their perceived value to collectors. Despite a production cost of $200 per piece, the market's high regard for her work allows for a selling price upwards of $2,000, reflecting the premium that collectors are willing to pay for her artistry and reputation.

Competition-Based Pricing Strategy

Competition-based pricing involves setting prices in relation to those of competitors, considering the market rate for similar products. This strategy demands a keen understanding of the competitive landscape and may require flexibility in pricing to respond to market changes.

Application in Ceramics: Suitable for ceramics businesses operating in a highly competitive market where price differentiation is crucial for attracting customers. It's important for businesses using this strategy to maintain a clear understanding of their value proposition to avoid entering a price war that could erode profit margins.

Case Study: A manufacturer of ceramic tiles surveys the market to determine the average selling price of tiles with similar quality and design. Finding the average market price to be $5 per square foot, the manufacturer sets its price at $4.75 to attract price-sensitive customers while ensuring their costs are covered and a modest profit margin is maintained.

Hybrid Pricing Strategies

Many ceramics businesses find that a single pricing strategy does not fully address the complexities of the market. A hybrid approach, combining elements of cost-plus, value-based, and competition-based pricing, can offer greater flexibility and effectiveness.

Application in Ceramics: A ceramics studio produces a range of products from standard dinnerware to limited edition art pieces. For the standard range, a cost-plus approach ensures costs are covered. For limited edition pieces, a value-based strategy captures the premium customers are willing to pay for exclusivity. For products similar to those offered by competitors, a competition-based approach ensures market competitiveness.

Case Study: A studio diversifies its product line to include both utilitarian items and high-end artistic pieces. For the utilitarian line, they apply a cost-plus strategy, ensuring a consistent profit margin. For the artistic line, prices are set based on perceived value, taking into account the reputation of the artists and the uniqueness of each piece. Competitive pricing is used for items that directly compete with similar offerings in the market, ensuring the studio remains attractive to a broad customer base.

Pricing Challenges and Considerations in Ceramics

While the above strategies provide a framework for pricing, ceramics businesses face unique challenges. The cost of materials and labor can vary, the value of art is subjective, and market conditions fluctuate. Effective pricing requires ongoing market research, understanding customer perceptions, and flexibility to adjust prices as needed.

Further considerations include the impact of pricing on brand positioning, the potential for pricing to influence perceived quality, and the importance of transparency in pricing for building customer trust. Additionally, businesses must navigate the psychological aspects of pricing, such as price points and the use of discounts or promotions.

Pricing strategies in the ceramics industry must be as varied and nuanced as the products themselves. By understanding and applying cost-plus, value-based, and competition-based pricing strategies, ceramics businesses can navigate the complex landscape of market demands, production costs, and competitive pressures. A hybrid approach, tailored to the diverse range of products and their respective markets, can provide the flexibility needed to maximize profitability while ensuring customer satisfaction and loyalty. Ultimately, the art of pricing ceramics lies in balancing the tangible costs of production with the intangible value of art, craftsmanship, and brand, crafting a strategy that resonates with the market and sustains the business's growth.

ppp

Summary

"Pricing Strategies for Ceramics Products" delves into an examination of various pricing models and their relevance to the ceramics industry, offering insights into cost-plus, value-based, and competition-based strategies. The cost-plus model focuses on covering production costs and adding a markup for profit, suitable for ensuring financial sustainability. Value-based pricing, on the other hand, assesses the perceived value of the ceramics to the customer, allowing artists to capture the premium associated with unique designs or heritage. Competition-based pricing considers the pricing strategies of peers within the market, helping ceramics businesses to position themselves competitively. This comprehensive analysis guides ceramicists and entrepreneurs in selecting the most appropriate pricing strategy, taking into account the unique characteristics of their products and market dynamics. By applying these models thoughtfully, ceramics businesses can optimize their pricing to reflect the quality and craftsmanship of their products while maximizing profitability and market share.

ppp

SIX

MARKET ANALYSIS FOR CERAMICS

How to conduct market research to inform pricing and product development decisions.

Market analysis is an essential component of running a successful ceramics business. By thoroughly understanding the market, ceramics artists and manufacturers can make informed decisions about pricing, product development, and marketing strategies. This chapter provides a comprehensive guide on conducting market research in the ceramics industry, ensuring businesses can identify opportunities, understand consumer preferences, and navigate the competitive landscape effectively.

Understanding the Ceramics Market

The ceramics market is diverse, encompassing everything from functional tableware and decorative pieces to industrial ceramics and art. Each segment has its own target audience, trends, and competitive dynamics. Initially, businesses must define their niche within the broader market to focus their research efforts effectively.

Conducting Market Research: A Step-by-Step Guide

1. Define Your Objectives

Start by clearly defining the objectives of your market research. Are you looking to enter a new market segment, assess the feasibility of a new product, or understand pricing strategies within your niche? Specific objectives will guide your research process and help you gather relevant information.

2. Segment Your Market

Break down the market into segments based on demographics (age, gender, income level), psychographics (lifestyle, values, interests), and behaviors (purchase habits, brand loyalty). This segmentation will enable you to identify your target customer groups more clearly.

3. Analyze Industry Trends

Stay abreast of trends in the ceramics industry that could impact your business. This includes technological advancements, shifts in consumer preferences, and changes in the regulatory environment. Trade publications, industry reports, and exhibitions can be valuable sources of information.

4. Evaluate the Competition

Identifying and analyzing your competitors is crucial. Look at their product offerings, pricing strategies, marketing approaches, and market positioning. This analysis can reveal gaps in the market, highlight best practices, and help you position your products effectively.

5. Gather Consumer Insights

Understanding your customers is key to successful product development and pricing. Conduct surveys, focus groups, or one-on-one interviews to gather insights into consumer needs, preferences, and perceptions. Social media and online forums can also be rich sources of customer feedback.

6. Assess the External Environment

Consider factors outside your control that could impact your market. This includes economic conditions, cultural trends, and technological changes. A SWOT analysis (Strengths, Weaknesses, Opportunities, Threats) can help you assess these external factors in relation to your business.

7. Analyze Your Findings

With data in hand, analyze your findings to draw actionable insights. Look for patterns in consumer behavior, unmet needs in the market, and opportunities for differentiation. This analysis will inform your decisions on product development, pricing, and marketing strategies.

Case Studies

To illustrate the application of market analysis in the ceramics industry, let's explore two case studies:

Case Study 1: Launching a New Line of Eco-Friendly Ceramics

A ceramics studio aimed to launch a new line of eco-friendly tableware. They conducted market research to assess consumer interest in sustainable products, analyze the competitive landscape for eco-friendly ceramics, and determine optimal pricing strategies.

Their research involved:

Surveys among potential customers to gauge interest in eco-friendly tableware.

Competitor analysis to understand how similar products were marketed and priced.

Trend analysis to identify growing consumer interest in sustainability.

The findings revealed a strong market demand for sustainable products, but with a significant emphasis on aesthetics and functionality. The studio decided to focus on developing a line that combined eco-friendly materials with contemporary designs, positioning their products at a premium price point to reflect their unique value proposition.

Case Study 2: Expanding into the Online Market

An established ceramics manufacturer traditionally sold products through retail partners. To explore opportunities for direct-to-consumer sales, they conducted market research focused on online buying behaviors within their target demographic. The research steps included:

Analyzing online search trends to understand consumer interest in ceramics.

Evaluating the online presence of competitors, including website design and e-commerce capabilities.

Gathering customer feedback on preferences for online shopping, including shipping options and return policies.

The research highlighted a growing trend towards online shopping for home decor items, including ceramics. The manufacturer decided to launch an e-commerce platform, focusing on user experience, high-quality product images, and storytelling to differentiate their brand. They also implemented a targeted digital marketing campaign to drive traffic to the new online store.

Leveraging Market Analysis for Strategic Decisions

The insights gained from market analysis are invaluable for making informed strategic decisions. In the case of the eco-friendly ceramics studio, market research informed not only product development but also pricing and marketing strategies. For the manufacturer expanding online, insights into consumer behavior guided the design of their e-commerce platform and marketing efforts.

Conducting thorough market analysis is critical for the success of ceramics businesses. By understanding market dynamics, consumer preferences, and the competitive landscape, businesses can make informed decisions that drive growth and profitability. Whether launching a new product line, entering a new market, or refining pricing strategies, market research provides the foundation for strategic decision-making. In the ever-evolving ceramics industry, staying attuned to the market through ongoing research is key to maintaining a competitive edge.

Summary

"Market Analysis for Ceramics" outlines the essential steps for conducting market research to guide pricing and product development in the ceramics industry. It emphasizes the importance of understanding consumer preferences, market trends, and competitive dynamics. The guide suggests methods for gathering data, such as surveys, interviews, and analysis of industry reports, to gain insights into what drives customer decisions and identifies gaps in the market. Additionally, it discusses how to evaluate the competitive landscape, assessing the strengths and weaknesses of competitors' offerings. This comprehensive approach to market analysis enables ceramics entrepreneurs to make informed decisions, tailoring their products and pricing strategies to meet market demands effectively and capitalize on emerging opportunities, thereby enhancing their competitiveness and fostering business growth.

ᐅᐅᐅ

SEVEN

Understanding and Applying Overhead Costs

Detailed exploration of overhead costs in ceramics businesses and strategies for effective allocation.

Overhead costs, while not directly linked to the production of ceramics, are critical to the operation of a ceramics business. These costs encompass expenses such as rent, utilities, marketing, salaries of non-production staff, equipment maintenance, and insurance. Understanding and efficiently managing these costs is crucial for the financial health and competitiveness of a ceramics business. Here Let's discuss the nature of overhead costs in the ceramics industry and outlines strategies for their effective allocation and management.

Understanding Overhead Costs

Overhead costs can be broadly classified into two categories: fixed and variable. Fixed overhead costs, such as rent and salaries of administrative staff, do not change with the level of production.

Variable overhead costs, such as utility bills or marketing expenses, can fluctuate based on production volume and other factors. For ceramics businesses, accurately categorizing and tracking these costs is the first step toward effective management.

Allocating Overhead Costs

The allocation of overhead costs to products is essential for accurately determining the cost of production and setting appropriate prices. There are several methods to allocate overhead costs, each with its strengths and nuances:

Direct Labor Hours: This method allocates overhead based on the number of labor hours spent on each product. It's suitable for labor-intensive ceramics operations where labor hours are a significant cost driver.

Machine Hours: In ceramics businesses that rely heavily on equipment, such as kilns, allocating overhead costs based on machine hours can be more accurate.

Direct Material Costs: Some businesses may allocate overhead based on the direct material costs of each product, which can be appropriate when material costs significantly drive overall costs.

Activity-Based Costing (ABC): ABC is a more detailed method that assigns overhead costs to products based on the activities that incur those costs. This method can be particularly useful for ceramics businesses with diverse product lines requiring different processes and resources.

Managing Overhead Costs

Effectively managing overhead costs involves both minimizing unnecessary expenses and strategically investing in areas that add value to the business. Strategies for managing overhead costs include:

Regular Review and Analysis: Continuously monitor overhead costs and analyze them in relation to production volumes and revenues. This ongoing review can help identify trends, inefficiencies, and opportunities for cost savings.

Negotiate with Suppliers: Regularly review contracts and negotiate with suppliers for better terms on raw materials, utilities, and services. Bulk purchasing and long-term contracts can lead to significant savings.

Energy Efficiency: Ceramics businesses, especially those using kilns, can incur high energy costs. Investing in energy-efficient kilns and optimizing firing schedules can reduce these expenses.

Outsourcing Non-Core Activities: Evaluate the cost-effectiveness of outsourcing non-core activities, such as marketing or logistics, which may be performed more efficiently by specialists.

Leveraging Technology: Implementing software solutions for inventory management, accounting, and customer relationship management can streamline operations and reduce administrative costs.

Case Studies

Case Study 1: Pottery Studio Reduces Energy Costs

A small pottery studio identified energy costs as its most significant variable overhead. By investing in a more energy-efficient kiln and optimizing firing schedules to maximize each firing's load, the studio significantly reduced its energy bills. The studio also switched to LED lighting and implemented energy-saving practices throughout its operations, further reducing its overhead costs.

Case Study 2: Manufacturer Implements ABC Costing

A ceramics manufacturer producing a wide range of products implemented activity-based costing to gain a better understanding of its overhead costs. By identifying and analyzing the activities that drove overhead costs, the manufacturer was able to allocate costs more accurately to each product line. This detailed analysis revealed that certain low-volume, high-complexity products were not as profitable as previously thought, leading to strategic adjustments in pricing and production focus.

Strategies for Effective Overhead Allocation

Understand Your Processes: Conduct a thorough analysis of your production processes to identify the primary drivers of overhead costs. This understanding is crucial for selecting the most appropriate allocation method.

Choose the Right Allocation Base: Select an allocation base that closely correlates with the incurrence of overhead costs. This alignment ensures that overhead costs are allocated fairly and accurately to products.

Implement ABC Where Feasible: Although more complex, activity-based costing can provide deeper insights into the true cost of production, especially for businesses with diverse products and processes.

Use Technology to Track Costs: Utilize accounting and business management software to track and allocate overhead costs accurately. These tools can automate the allocation process and provide valuable data for analysis.

Overhead costs play a significant role in the financial structure of ceramics businesses. Understanding, allocating, and managing these costs effectively is crucial for accurate product costing, competitive pricing, and overall business sustainability. By applying the strategies outlined in this chapter, ceramics businesses can gain greater control over their overhead costs, make more informed decisions, and enhance their profitability. Through regular review, strategic allocation, and targeted management efforts, businesses can turn the challenge of overhead costs into an opportunity for efficiency and growth.

ﬞ ﬞ ﬞ

Summary

"Understanding and Applying Overhead Costs" offers a detailed exploration of the often-overlooked aspect of running a ceramics business: the overhead costs. This essential guide lays out the types of overheads – from studio rental and utilities to marketing and administrative expenses – that ceramicists face. More importantly, it presents strategies for effectively allocating these costs to ensure that they are accurately reflected in the pricing of ceramics products. By providing a comprehensive understanding of overhead costs, this resource aids ceramics entrepreneurs in developing a more nuanced financial strategy. It highlights the importance of not just covering these costs but also strategically managing them to improve overall business efficiency and profitability. Through practical advice and real-world examples, ceramicists are equipped with the knowledge to make informed decisions about cost control and pricing, ensuring their business's sustainability and growth in the competitive ceramics market.

ᗡᗡᗡ

EIGHT

INVENTORY MANAGEMENT AND COSTING

Techniques for managing ceramics inventory, including LIFO, FIFO, and weighted average methods.

Inventory management is a critical aspect of running a successful ceramics business, impacting both the operational efficiency and financial health of the enterprise. Proper management of inventory ensures that ceramics businesses can meet demand without holding excessive stock, which ties up capital and incurs storage costs. Additionally, accurate inventory costing is essential for financial reporting and decision-making.

Here we will explore effective techniques for managing and costing inventory in the ceramics industry, focusing on the Last-In, First-Out (LIFO), First-In, First-Out (FIFO), and weighted average methods.

Understanding Inventory in Ceramics Businesses

Inventory in ceramics businesses typically includes raw materials (such as clay, glazes, and paints), work-in-progress (items that are in various stages of production), and finished goods (completed items ready for sale). Effective inventory management strategies must consider the unique characteristics of these items, including the shelf life of raw materials, the time required for production, and the storage requirements for finished goods.

Inventory Management Techniques

Effective inventory management involves balancing the need to meet customer demand with the goal of minimizing holding costs. Techniques commonly used in the ceramics industry include:

Just-In-Time (JIT) Inventory: This strategy aims to reduce inventory levels by ordering and producing goods only as needed. While JIT can significantly reduce storage costs and minimize waste, it requires accurate demand forecasting and reliable suppliers.

Economic Order Quantity (EOQ): EOQ is a formula used to determine the optimal order quantity that minimizes the total costs of ordering and holding inventory. This approach can help ceramics businesses reduce costs while ensuring sufficient materials are on hand.

ABC Analysis: This technique involves categorizing inventory into three categories (A, B, and C) based on their importance or value to the business. Category A items are the most valuable and are managed more closely, while Category C items are the least valuable and require simpler controls.

Inventory Costing Methods

Accurate inventory costing is crucial for determining the cost of goods sold (COGS) and gross profit. The three primary costing methods used in inventory management are LIFO, FIFO, and the weighted average method.

Last-In, First-Out (LIFO)

LIFO assumes that the most recently acquired items are sold first. This method can be beneficial in times of rising prices, as it matches current costs with current revenues, potentially leading to a lower taxable income.

However, LIFO can also result in older stock being left unsold, which may not be ideal for ceramics with changing styles or materials that deteriorate over time.

First-In, First-Out (FIFO)

FIFO assumes that the oldest items in inventory are sold first. This method is intuitive and mirrors the natural flow of goods in many businesses. FIFO can lead to higher taxable income in periods of inflation, as the cost of older, cheaper goods is matched with current revenues. However, it ensures that inventory valuation reflects the cost of replacing items at current prices.

Weighted Average Method

The weighted average method calculates the cost of inventory based on the average cost of all items in stock, adjusted for purchases during the period. This approach smooths out price fluctuations over time and is straightforward to implement. However, it may not reflect the actual flow of goods as accurately as LIFO or FIFO.

Case Studies in Ceramics Inventory Management

Case Study 1: Implementing JIT in a Pottery Studio

A small pottery studio implemented a JIT inventory system to manage its raw materials. By closely monitoring demand and working with reliable suppliers, the studio was able to order clay and glazes just in time for production cycles, significantly reducing storage needs and minimizing the risk of material spoilage. This strategy required meticulous planning and communication but resulted in lower overhead costs and increased operational efficiency.

Case Study 2: Adopting FIFO in a Ceramic Tile Manufacturer

A ceramic tile manufacturer adopted the FIFO method for its inventory of finished goods. This approach ensured that older designs were sold first, reducing the risk of obsolescence and ensuring that inventory valuation accurately reflected replacement costs. By implementing FIFO, the manufacturer improved its inventory turnover rate and ensured that its financial statements accurately reflected the cost of goods sold.

Strategies for Effective Inventory Management and Costing

Accurate Demand Forecasting: Use historical sales data, market trends, and seasonal patterns to forecast demand accurately. This information is crucial for implementing JIT and determining EOQ.

Reliable Supplier Relationships: Develop strong relationships with suppliers to ensure timely delivery of materials, which is especially important for JIT inventory systems.

Regular Inventory Audits: Conduct physical counts of inventory regularly to verify records and adjust for discrepancies. This practice is essential for maintaining accurate inventory levels and financial records.

Use of Technology: Implement inventory management software to track inventory levels, forecast demand, and streamline the ordering process. Technology can also assist in applying the chosen costing method consistently.

Continuous Improvement: Regularly review and adjust inventory management and costing strategies based on operational performance and changing market conditions. Continuous improvement can lead to more efficient operations and improved financial performance.

Effective inventory management and accurate costing are foundational to the success of ceramics businesses. By understanding and applying appropriate techniques for managing inventory—such as JIT, EOQ, and ABC analysis—and by choosing the most suitable costing method—be it LIFO, FIFO, or the weighted average method—ceramics businesses can optimize their operations, reduce costs, and improve profitability. The implementation of these strategies, supported by accurate demand forecasting, reliable supplier relationships, and the use of technology, will enable ceramics businesses to navigate the challenges of inventory management and thrive in a competitive market.

ϷϷϷ

Summary

"Inventory Management and Costing" delves into the crucial aspect of managing ceramics inventory, presenting a clear and concise overview of techniques such as Last In, First Out (LIFO), First In, First Out (FIFO), and the weighted average method. These inventory costing methods offer different approaches to valuing stock and cost of goods sold, each with its implications for financial reporting and tax purposes. The guide emphasizes the importance of choosing the right method to suit the specific needs and operational dynamics of a ceramics business. By adopting an effective inventory management and costing strategy, ceramics businesses can achieve more accurate financial records, optimize stock levels, and improve cash flow management. This resource equips ceramics entrepreneurs with the knowledge to make informed decisions about inventory practices, ultimately enhancing profitability and operational efficiency.

ppp

NINE

Financial Planning for Ceramics Entrepreneurs

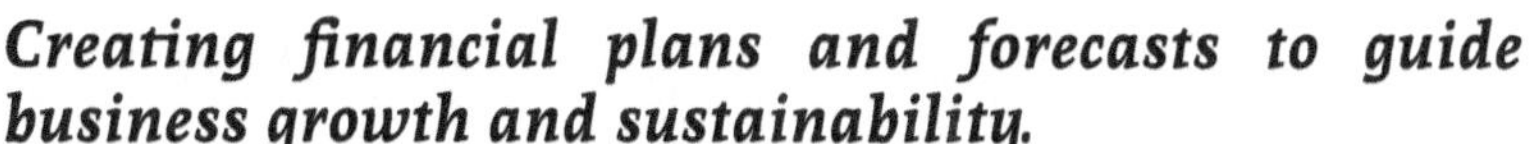

Creating financial plans and forecasts to guide business growth and sustainability.

Financial planning is a critical component for ceramics entrepreneurs aiming to navigate their business toward growth and sustainability. A comprehensive financial plan serves as a roadmap, outlining the business's financial goals, strategies to achieve them, and the resources required. It involves detailed forecasting, budgeting, and financial analysis, enabling entrepreneurs to make informed decisions, secure funding, and manage risks effectively.

Let's understand the key elements of financial planning for ceramics entrepreneurs, offering insights into creating robust financial plans and forecasts.

Understanding the Importance of Financial Planning

Financial planning is essential for ceramics businesses of all sizes. It helps entrepreneurs:

Identify financial goals: Clear goals guide the direction of the business, from short-term objectives like purchasing new equipment to long-term aspirations such as expanding the product line.

Allocate resources efficiently: A financial plan outlines how resources will be used, ensuring that investments are made in areas that maximize returns.

Secure financing: Detailed financial plans are crucial for attracting investors or securing loans, as they demonstrate the viability and future profitability of the business.

Manage cash flow: Effective financial planning includes cash flow management strategies to ensure the business can meet its obligations and invest in growth opportunities.

Anticipate and mitigate risks: Financial forecasts help identify potential financial challenges, allowing businesses to develop strategies to address them proactively.

Components of a Financial Plan

A comprehensive financial plan for a ceramics business should include the following components:

Executive Summary: An overview of the business and its financial goals, serving as an introduction to the financial plan.

Market Analysis: Insights into the ceramics market, including target demographics, competition, and pricing strategies, providing context for the financial projections.

Sales Forecast: An estimate of future sales based on market analysis, historical sales data, and marketing strategies. This forecast is crucial for predicting revenue and planning production.

Expense Budget: A detailed breakdown of expected costs, including both fixed costs (e.g., rent, salaries) and variable costs (e.g., materials, shipping). This budget is essential for managing expenses and maintaining profitability.

Cash Flow Projection: A forecast of cash inflows and outflows over a specific period, highlighting when the business might face cash shortages and need additional funding.

Profit and Loss Projection: An estimate of the business's profitability, showing expected revenues, costs, and the resulting net profit or loss.

Balance Sheet Projection: A snapshot of the business's financial position at a future point in time, including assets, liabilities, and equity.

Break-even Analysis: Calculation of the point at which total revenues equal total costs, indicating the minimum sales needed to cover expenses.

Creating Financial Forecasts

Developing accurate financial forecasts is challenging but essential. These tips can help ceramics entrepreneurs create realistic and useful forecasts:

Start with sales forecasts: Use historical sales data, market trends, and any planned marketing activities to estimate future sales. Be conservative to avoid overestimating revenue.

Estimate costs realistically: Review historical expense data and consider any expected changes, such as increases in material costs or plans for expansion, to forecast future expenses accurately.

Project cash flow: Combine sales forecasts and expense estimates to project cash flow. Pay special attention to seasonal variations in sales and expenses, which can significantly impact cash flow.

Review and adjust regularly: Financial forecasts are based on assumptions that can change. Regularly review and update your forecasts to reflect the latest data and market conditions.

Financial Planning Strategies for Ceramics Entrepreneurs

Implementing effective financial planning strategies can significantly impact the success of a ceramics business. Consider the following strategies:

Diversify revenue streams: Explore different revenue streams, such as custom commissions, workshops, or online sales, to reduce reliance on a single source of income.

Manage inventory efficiently: Implement inventory management techniques to minimize storage costs and reduce the risk of excess stock.

Optimize pricing: Regularly review and adjust pricing based on cost analysis, market demand, and competitive positioning to ensure profitability.

Control costs: Continuously seek ways to reduce costs without compromising quality, such as negotiating better terms with suppliers or investing in energy-efficient equipment.

Plan for contingencies: Set aside a financial buffer to deal with unexpected expenses or downturns in sales, ensuring the business can weather financial challenges.

Case Study: Financial Planning in Action

A small ceramics studio specializing in handmade pottery implemented a robust financial plan to support its growth ambitions. The studio conducted a thorough market analysis to understand its target customers and competition, informing its pricing and marketing strategies.

Sales forecasts were based on historical sales data and planned marketing initiatives, while expense budgets were developed using detailed cost analysis.

The financial plan included cash flow projections highlighting the need for additional funding to purchase a new kiln and expand the studio space. With this plan, the studio successfully secured a loan, providing the necessary capital for growth.

Regularly reviewing and adjusting its financial forecasts allowed the studio to navigate unexpected challenges, such as a rise in material costs, without compromising its growth trajectory.

Financial planning is a dynamic and ongoing process that is crucial for the success and sustainability of ceramics businesses. By understanding the market, accurately forecasting financial performance, and implementing effective management strategies, ceramics entrepreneurs can guide their businesses toward growth and profitability.

A comprehensive financial plan not only helps in securing funding and managing risks but also provides a clear vision for the future, enabling entrepreneurs to make informed decisions and adapt to changing market conditions.

ᗐᗐᗐ

Summary

"Financial Planning for Ceramics Entrepreneurs" offers a comprehensive guide to creating robust financial plans and forecasts, tailored specifically for those in the ceramics industry. This vital resource emphasizes the importance of financial planning in guiding business growth and ensuring sustainability. It outlines how to construct detailed financial models, including revenue projections, expense forecasts, and cash flow analysis, tailored to the unique aspects of ceramics production and sales. By integrating market analysis, cost structures, and pricing strategies, ceramics entrepreneurs can develop realistic and actionable financial forecasts. This guide also covers the strategic use of these financial plans to secure funding, manage risks, and make informed business decisions. Through practical advice and step-by-step instructions, "Financial Planning for Ceramics Entrepreneurs" empowers artists and business owners to lay a strong financial foundation for their ventures, aiming for long-term success and stability in the vibrant field of ceramics.

ƿƿƿ

TEN

Investment Appraisal in the Ceramics Industry

Methods for evaluating investment opportunities, including payback period, NPV, and IRR.

Investment appraisal is a crucial aspect of strategic decision-making in the ceramics industry, enabling businesses to evaluate the viability and profitability of potential investments.

Whether considering the purchase of new kilns, expanding production facilities, or venturing into new markets, ceramics entrepreneurs must assess the financial implications of such investments to ensure they contribute positively to the business's growth and sustainability.

In this section we will discuss the key methods of investment appraisal—payback period, Net Present Value (NPV), and Internal Rate of Return (IRR)—and their application within the ceramics industry.

Understanding Investment Appraisal

Investment appraisal involves analyzing prospective investments to determine their financial worthiness. The process helps businesses allocate limited resources to projects with the highest potential for returns, minimizing risks and maximizing profitability. In the context of the ceramics industry, where investments often involve significant capital expenditures and long-term commitments, a thorough appraisal is indispensable.

Payback Period

The payback period method calculates the time required for an investment to generate cash flows sufficient to recover the initial outlay. It is a simple and straightforward approach that helps businesses assess the risk associated with an investment, with shorter payback periods typically perceived as less risky.

Application in Ceramics: Consider a ceramics studio planning to invest in a new kiln costing $10,000, expecting to increase production efficiency and generate an additional $2,500 in cash flow annually. The payback period would be 4 years ($10,000 / $2,500), suggesting how long the studio must wait to recoup its investment.

Advantages: Simplicity and ease of calculation.

Limitations: Ignores the time value of money and cash flows beyond the payback period.

Net Present Value (NPV)

NPV calculates the present value of future cash flows generated by an investment, discounted back to their value today, minus the initial investment cost. A positive NPV indicates that the investment is expected to generate more value than the cost, making it a potentially good investment.

Application in Ceramics: If the same ceramics studio expects the new kiln to generate varying annual cash flows over five years, it would discount those cash flows to their present value using a discount rate (often the cost of capital or required rate of return) and subtract the initial investment. If the result is positive, the investment is financially viable.

Advantages: Accounts for the time value of money and considers the entire life of the investment.

Limitations: Requires an estimate of future cash flows and an appropriate discount rate, both of which can be uncertain.

Internal Rate of Return (IRR)

IRR is the discount rate that makes the NPV of an investment zero. In other words, it is the rate of return at which the present value of an investment's cash inflows equals the present value of its outflows. Investments with an IRR exceeding the required rate of return or cost of capital are generally considered attractive.

Application in Ceramics: If the investment in the new kiln results in an IRR of 12%, and the studio's cost of capital is 8%, the investment would be considered attractive, as it promises a return higher than the minimum required.

Advantages: Provides a clear percentage rate of return, making it easy to compare with the cost of capital or other investment opportunities.

Limitations: Can give misleading results if used alone for mutually exclusive projects or if the cash flows change sign multiple times over the investment's lifespan.

Strategic Considerations in Investment Appraisal

In the ceramics industry, investment decisions often go beyond financial metrics, encompassing strategic considerations such as:

Market Expansion: Investments that open new markets or expand the studio's customer base might justify longer payback periods or lower initial returns.

Product Development: Investing in new product lines or innovative production techniques can offer competitive advantages, even if the direct financial return is not immediate.

Sustainability: Investments in energy-efficient kilns or sustainable materials, though potentially costly upfront, may align with long-term brand values and customer expectations, offering intangible benefits.

Case Study: Expansion of a Ceramics Manufacturing Facility

A ceramics manufacturer considering an expansion of its production facility conducted an investment appraisal using NPV and IRR methods. The expansion involved an initial investment of $500,000, expected to generate additional annual cash flows of $120,000 over ten years. Using a discount rate of 10%, the NPV was calculated to be positive, indicating that the present value of future cash flows exceeded the investment cost. The IRR was found to be

12%, higher than the company's cost of capital.

Based on these financial metrics, the expansion appeared to be a sound investment. However, the decision was also influenced by strategic considerations, such as the ability to meet growing demand, reduce reliance on external suppliers, and enhance the company's market position. The comprehensive appraisal, combining financial analysis with strategic insights, led to a confident decision to proceed with the expansion.

Investment appraisal is an indispensable tool for ceramics entrepreneurs, enabling the thorough evaluation of investment opportunities and informed decision-making. By applying methods such as payback period, net present value (NPV), and internal rate of return (IRR), entrepreneurs can assess the feasibility and potential returns of various investment projects. This chapter has provided a comprehensive overview of investment appraisal techniques, highlighting their strengths, limitations, and practical applications in the ceramics industry.

Through the case studies presented, we have witnessed how ceramics businesses have utilized investment appraisal to guide strategic investments and drive growth. From upgrading production facilities to expanding into new markets, entrepreneurs have leveraged these tools to make sound financial decisions that align with their business objectives.

As we conclude our exploration of investment appraisal in the ceramics industry, it is evident that the ability to evaluate investment opportunities rigorously is essential for long-term success. By embracing these techniques and integrating them into their decision-making processes, entrepreneurs can mitigate risks, optimize resource allocation, and maximize returns on investment.

Looking ahead, the ceramics industry is poised for continued evolution and innovation. As new technologies emerge, consumer preferences evolve, and market dynamics shift, the need for robust investment appraisal practices will remain paramount. By staying informed, adaptable, and forward-thinking, ceramics entrepreneurs can navigate the complexities of the investment landscape and capitalize on emerging opportunities, driving sustainable growth and prosperity in the industry for years to come.

❧❧❧

Summary

"Investment Appraisal in the Ceramics Industry" provides a thorough examination of methods for evaluating investment opportunities within the ceramics sector. It introduces readers to key financial metrics such as the payback period, Net Present Value (NPV), and Internal Rate of Return (IRR), explaining their significance and application in making informed investment decisions. The guide emphasizes the importance of these appraisal methods in assessing the viability and potential returns of investments, whether in new equipment, technology, or expansion projects. By applying these tools, ceramics entrepreneurs can systematically analyze the financial implications of their investment choices, ensuring that they contribute positively to the business's growth and profitability. This resource aims to equip ceramics business owners with the knowledge to navigate investment opportunities confidently, fostering strategic development and long-term success in the industry.

ppp

ELEVEN

BREAK-EVEN ANALYSIS FOR CERAMICS PRODUCTS

Tools and strategies for determining the break-even point for various ceramics products.

Break-even analysis is a pivotal tool for ceramics businesses, providing clarity on the viability of their products by determining the point at which sales cover all costs, resulting in neither profit nor loss. This analysis is crucial for pricing strategies, cost management, and financial planning, helping entrepreneurs make informed decisions about product lines, production volumes, and market entry.

This chapter examines the intricacies of break-even analysis, elucidating the methodology, tools, and strategies crafted specifically for the ceramics industry.

Understanding Break-even Analysis

The break-even point (BEP) is calculated by identifying the intersection where total revenues equal total costs. This concept is vital for ceramics entrepreneurs who need to understand how many units of their product must be sold at a given price to cover their costs, including both fixed and variable expenses.

Components of Break-even Analysis

Fixed Costs: These are costs that do not change with the level of production or sales, such as rent, salaries of permanent staff, and depreciation of equipment. Accurately identifying and quantifying fixed costs is the first step in break-even analysis.

Variable Costs: Variable costs fluctuate with production volume, including costs for materials (clay, glazes), direct labor (wages of artisans per piece), and utilities directly tied to production activities.

Sale Price per Unit: This is the price at which each ceramic piece is sold. Setting this price involves considering the cost of production, market conditions, and the perceived value of the product.

Calculating the Break-even Point

The break-even point can be calculated using the formula:

BEP (units)
=
Fixed Costs
Sale Price per Unit
−
Variable Cost per Unit

BEP (units)=

Sale Price per Unit–Variable Cost per Unit

Fixed Costs

This formula reveals the number of units that must be sold to cover all costs. It's a critical figure for ceramics businesses, indicating the minimum production and sales target needed to avoid losses.

Practical Application in the Ceramics Industry

Example 1: Handmade Pottery Studio

A studio producing handmade pottery faces fixed costs of $20,000 per year, which include studio rent, insurance, and salaries for permanent staff. The variable cost to produce one pot is $10, including clay, glazes, and the energy cost for firing. If the sale price per pot is set at $30, the break-even point would be:

$$\text{BEP (units)} = \frac{\$20,000}{\$30 - \$10} = 1,000 \text{ pots}$$

This means the studio must sell at least 1,000 pots annually to cover all costs.

Example 2: Ceramic Sculpture Artist

A ceramic sculpture artist with fixed costs of $15,000 annually and variable costs of $50 per sculpture (materials and studio utilities) plans to sell sculptures for $200 each. The break-even point calculation would be:

$$\text{BEP (units)} = \frac{\$15,000}{\$200 - \$50} = 100 \text{ sculptures}$$

The artist needs to sell at least 100 sculptures per year to break even.

Strategies for Using Break-even Analysis

Pricing Decisions: Break-even analysis helps ceramics businesses set prices that not only cover costs but also align with market conditions and profitability goals.

Cost Management: Identifying the break-even point highlights the importance of managing fixed and variable costs. Reducing costs can lower the break-even point, making the business more resilient to sales fluctuations.

Product Viability: Before introducing a new product line, break-even analysis can determine its financial viability by estimating the required sales volume to cover costs.

Financial Planning and Forecasting: Understanding the break-even point aids in forecasting revenue, planning for growth, and making informed investment decisions.

Tools for Break-even Analysis

Spreadsheets: Excel or similar spreadsheet software can be powerful tools for conducting break-even analysis, allowing for the easy adjustment of variables (costs, prices, and sales volumes) to see their impact on the break-even point.

Break-even Analysis Software: There are dedicated software tools and apps designed for break-even analysis that offer more functionality and can incorporate more complex variables.

Graphical Methods: Visual representation of break-even analysis can help businesses understand the relationship between costs, volume, and profits at different sales levels, providing a clear picture of financial dynamics.

Adjusting to Market Dynamics

Ceramics businesses must remain flexible and responsive to market changes. Regularly updating break-even analysis to reflect shifts in costs, market demand, and competition is essential. Seasonal demand fluctuations, changes in supplier pricing, and evolving consumer preferences can all impact the break-even point, necessitating adjustments in pricing strategies and cost management practices.

Break-even analysis is an indispensable tool for ceramics businesses, providing critical insights into the financial underpinnings of product lines and guiding strategic decision-making. By accurately calculating and understanding the break-even point, ceramics entrepreneurs can make informed decisions about pricing, cost control, and product development.

Embracing this analysis as part of regular business planning ensures that ceramics businesses can navigate the challenges of the market, adapt to changing conditions, and pursue sustainable growth and profitability. Through diligent application and regular review of break-even analysis, ceramics businesses can position themselves for success in the competitive and ever-evolving ceramics industry.

ᗡᗡᗡ

Summary

"Break-even Analysis for Ceramics Products" offers a focused look at tools and strategies essential for determining the break-even point for various ceramics products. This crucial financial concept helps ceramics entrepreneurs understand at what point their product sales will cover all costs, setting a foundational benchmark for profitability. The guide explains how to calculate fixed and variable costs associated with ceramics production and how to apply these figures to find the break-even point for different products. It emphasizes the importance of this analysis in pricing strategies, product development, and financial planning. By mastering break-even analysis, ceramics business owners can make more informed decisions about scaling production, introducing new product lines, and adjusting pricing models to ensure sustainable growth and profitability in the competitive ceramics market.

᭞᭞᭞

TWELVE
Profit Maximization Techniques

Strategies for maximizing profitability through efficient production, cost control, and pricing adjustments.

Profit maximization is a primary goal for any business, including those in the ceramics industry. Achieving this goal requires a multifaceted approach, focusing on enhancing production efficiency, controlling costs, and making strategic pricing adjustments.

By implementing these strategies, ceramics businesses can improve their profit margins, ensuring long-term sustainability and growth. Let's go through various techniques for maximizing profitability, tailored to the unique aspects of ceramics production.

Enhancing Production Efficiency

Production efficiency is crucial for maximizing profitability in ceramics businesses. It involves optimizing the production process to reduce waste, increase output, and maintain high-quality standards.

Lean Manufacturing Principles: Adopting lean manufacturing principles can help identify and eliminate waste in the production process, including excess inventory, overproduction, and defects. Techniques such as value stream mapping can provide insights into the production flow and identify areas for improvement.

Automation and Technology: Investing in automation and advanced technology can significantly enhance production efficiency. For example, automated kilns with precise temperature control can improve firing consistency, reduce defects, and save energy.

Skill Development and Training: Providing ongoing training for artisans and staff can improve skill levels, leading to faster production times and higher-quality outputs. Specialized training in techniques like glazing and hand-building can also expand the range of products offered.

Process Standardization: Standardizing production processes, from raw material preparation to final glazing, can reduce variability and increase efficiency. Creating detailed process guides and checklists can help maintain consistent quality and reduce errors.

Cost Control Strategies

Effective cost control is essential for maximizing profitability. By closely monitoring and managing costs, ceramics businesses can maintain competitive pricing while ensuring a healthy profit margin.

Raw Material Procurement: Securing raw materials at the best possible prices without compromising quality is vital. This may involve negotiating contracts with suppliers, buying in bulk, or exploring alternative materials that offer cost savings.

Energy Efficiency: For ceramics businesses, energy costs, especially for kiln firing, can be significant. Investing in energy-efficient kilns, optimizing firing schedules, and exploring renewable energy sources can reduce these costs.

Waste Reduction: Minimizing waste not only reduces material costs but also environmental impact. Implementing recycling programs for clay and glaze, and reusing materials whenever possible, can contribute to cost savings.

Overhead Cost Management: Regularly reviewing overhead costs, such as rent, utilities, and administrative expenses, can identify opportunities for savings. For instance, shifting to a more cost-effective location or reducing non-essential expenses can lower overhead.

Pricing Adjustments

Pricing strategies play a critical role in profitability. The right pricing not only covers costs but also reflects the value of the products to customers.

Cost-Plus Pricing: This strategy involves adding a markup to the cost of production to ensure a profit. While straightforward, it's essential to consider market acceptance and competitor pricing to avoid overpricing.

Value-Based Pricing: Setting prices based on the perceived value of the ceramics to customers can maximize profitability, especially for unique or artisanal pieces. This requires understanding customer preferences and the factors they value, such as design, craftsmanship, and brand reputation.

Dynamic Pricing: Adjusting prices in response to demand, competition, and market conditions can optimize profits. For example, limited-edition pieces may command higher prices due to their exclusivity.

Psychological Pricing: Implementing pricing strategies that appeal to customer psychology, such as pricing items just below a round number ($19.99 instead of $20), can increase sales while maintaining profitability.

Case Study: Maximizing Profitability in a Ceramics Studio

A mid-sized ceramics studio specializing in handmade tableware implemented several strategies to maximize its profitability. The studio adopted lean manufacturing principles, reorganizing its production floor to streamline the workflow and reduce movement. This reorganization cut production time by 15% and reduced breakage rates.

The studio also negotiated longer-term contracts with its clay and glaze suppliers, securing lower prices for bulk purchases. Additionally, it invested in an energy-efficient kiln, which reduced energy costs by 20% per firing cycle.

On the pricing front, the studio moved to a value-based pricing model for its signature line, highlighting the craftsmanship and unique designs in its marketing materials. This allowed for a 10% increase in prices without affecting sales volumes, reflecting customers' willingness to pay more for perceived value.

Finally, the studio implemented a cost-control dashboard to

monitor key expenses closely, including raw materials, energy, and overhead. This real-time monitoring enabled the studio to respond quickly to cost overruns, maintaining its profit margins.

Implementing Profit Maximization Strategies

Implementing these strategies requires careful planning and ongoing evaluation:

Conduct a thorough analysis of current production processes, costs, and pricing strategies to identify areas for improvement.

Set clear goals for efficiency improvements, cost reductions, and pricing adjustments, with specific, measurable targets.

Involve the team in the planning and implementation process, ensuring buy-in and encouraging innovative ideas for improvement.

Monitor progress regularly against the set goals, adjusting strategies as needed based on performance and market changes.

Maximizing profitability in the ceramics industry involves a balanced approach to enhancing production efficiency, controlling costs, and adjusting pricing strategies. By adopting lean manufacturing principles, investing in technology, negotiating better material prices, and understanding the market for strategic pricing, ceramics businesses can improve their profit margins. Regular analysis and adaptation to market conditions are crucial for sustaining profitability. Implementing these strategies not only ensures financial success but also supports the long-term growth and sustainability of ceramics businesses.

ᛋᛋᛋ

Summary

"Profit Maximization Techniques" presents a collection of strategies aimed at boosting the profitability of ceramics businesses through efficient production processes, stringent cost control measures, and strategic pricing adjustments. It delves into optimizing production workflows to reduce waste and increase output, ensuring that every step from clay preparation to glazing and firing is as efficient as possible. The guide also highlights the importance of controlling both fixed and variable costs, from negotiating better rates for materials to streamlining overhead expenses. Additionally, it explores various pricing strategies that reflect the value of the ceramics, catering to market demand while ensuring a healthy profit margin. By integrating these techniques, ceramics entrepreneurs can enhance their business's financial performance, driving growth and ensuring long-term sustainability in a competitive market landscape.

ᐁᐁᐁ

THIRTEEN

TAXATION AND ITS IMPACT ON CERAMICS BUSINESSES

Overview of tax considerations for ceramics businesses and strategies for tax optimization.

Taxation is an essential factor for ceramics businesses to consider, impacting everything from cash flow to business strategy. Understanding the nuances of tax obligations and leveraging strategies for tax optimization can significantly benefit a ceramics business's bottom line.

Understanding Tax Obligations

The first step in managing taxation is to understand the types of taxes that ceramics businesses might be subject to, which can vary by location and business structure. These taxes often include:

Income Tax: Taxes on profits generated by the business. Planning and timely reporting are crucial to manage income tax liabilities effectively.

Sales Tax: Collected from customers at the point of sale on taxable goods and services, then remitted to the tax authorities. Compliance involves accurate collection, reporting, and remittance.

Property Tax: For businesses that own property, such as a studio or retail space, property taxes are based on the assessed value of the property.

Payroll Taxes: If the business has employees, it is responsible for withholding payroll taxes from employees' wages and paying employer payroll taxes.

Self-Employment Taxes: For sole proprietors and partners, self-employment taxes cover Social Security and Medicare contributions.

Tax Optimization Strategies

Implementing strategies to manage and minimize tax liabilities can lead to significant savings for ceramics businesses. Key strategies include:

1. Choosing the Right Business Structure

The structure of a ceramics business (e.g., sole proprietorship, partnership, corporation) can significantly impact its tax obligations. Each structure has different tax rates, deductions, and filing requirements. Consulting with a tax professional can help determine the most tax-efficient structure for your business.

2. Taking Advantage of Tax Deductions and Credits

Many expenses associated with running a ceramics business are tax-deductible, including costs of materials, equipment, studio rent, utilities, and marketing expenses. Additionally, tax credits for activities such as research and development or investments in energy-efficient equipment can reduce tax liability. Keeping detailed records of all expenses and understanding which are deductible can maximize tax savings.

3. Implementing Effective Inventory Management

Inventory costs impact the taxable income of ceramics businesses. Adopting an inventory accounting method (e.g., FIFO, LIFO) that aligns with the business's financial strategy can influence reported income and tax liabilities.

4. Employing Retirement Savings Plans

For sole proprietors and small business owners, contributing to a retirement savings plan not only secures financial future but also offers immediate tax benefits, reducing taxable income.

5. Deferring Income and Accelerating Deductions

Strategically deferring income to the next tax year and accelerating deductions into the current tax year can reduce current year tax liabilities. This strategy requires careful planning to ensure cash flow needs are met.

6. Utilizing Loss Carryforwards and Carrybacks

Businesses experiencing losses can use those losses to offset taxable income in other years, either by carrying them back to previous years for a refund or carrying them forward to reduce future taxable income.

7. Staying Informed on Tax Law Changes

Tax laws and regulations are subject to change. Staying informed on current laws and upcoming changes is crucial for tax planning and compliance.

Case Study: Tax Optimization in Action

A mid-sized ceramics studio, structured as an LLC, navigated a challenging financial year by implementing several tax optimization strategies. Recognizing the importance of accurate record-keeping, the studio invested in accounting software to track expenses meticulously, ensuring all eligible deductions were captured.

They also consulted with a tax advisor to review their business structure, ultimately deciding to elect S corporation tax treatment to reduce self-employment tax liabilities.

To manage inventory costs effectively, the studio adopted the FIFO inventory accounting method, aligning with their strategy of using older materials first to minimize waste and reduce taxable income. Additionally, they accelerated purchases of new equipment into the current tax year to take advantage of immediate tax deductions and invested in a retirement savings plan for the owner, further reducing taxable income.

By deferring some income to the next tax year through strategic timing of sales and invoicing, the studio managed to balance its cash flow needs while minimizing its tax liability. They also kept abreast of tax law changes, taking advantage of a new tax credit for small businesses investing in health and safety improvements for their workspace.

Strategies for Ceramics Businesses

Engage a Tax Professional: Regular consultations with a tax advisor or accountant can help navigate the complexities of tax planning and compliance, ensuring that ceramics businesses take advantage of all available tax-saving opportunities.

Maintain Accurate and Detailed Financial Records: Keeping meticulous records of all transactions, expenses, and income is essential for accurate tax reporting and taking full advantage of deductions and credits.

Plan for Taxes Year-Round: Rather than treating taxes as a once-a-year event, integrate tax planning into the regular business planning process to identify opportunities for optimization and ensure compliance.

Educate Yourself and Stay Informed: While professional advice is invaluable, understanding the basics of tax law and staying informed about changes can help ceramics business owners make better financial decisions.

Taxation significantly impacts ceramics businesses, but with careful planning and strategic decision-making, it is possible to manage and optimize tax liabilities effectively.

By understanding their tax obligations, taking full advantage of deductions and credits, and employing strategies such as effective inventory management and income deferral, ceramics entrepreneurs can minimize their tax burden and enhance their business's profitability.

Engaging with tax professionals and maintaining accurate financial records are critical components of a successful tax strategy, ensuring compliance and financial health for the business. Through diligent tax planning and optimization, ceramics businesses can secure a more sustainable and profitable future.

❦❦❦

Summary

"Taxation and Its Impact on Ceramics Businesses" provides an essential overview of the tax considerations specific to the ceramics industry, alongside strategies for effective tax optimization. It covers the spectrum of taxes that ceramics businesses may encounter, from income and sales tax to import/ export duties, offering insights into how these can affect overall business operations and profitability. The guide emphasizes the importance of understanding the tax landscape to legally minimize tax liabilities, such as taking advantage of available deductions, credits, and incentives relevant to the ceramics sector. It also highlights the role of accurate record-keeping and strategic financial planning in managing tax obligations efficiently. By adopting the tax optimization strategies outlined, ceramics entrepreneurs can safeguard their margins, ensuring more of their revenue is invested back into the business to fuel growth and innovation.

▷▷▷

FOURTEEN

FINANCING OPTIONS FOR CERAMICS BUSINESSES

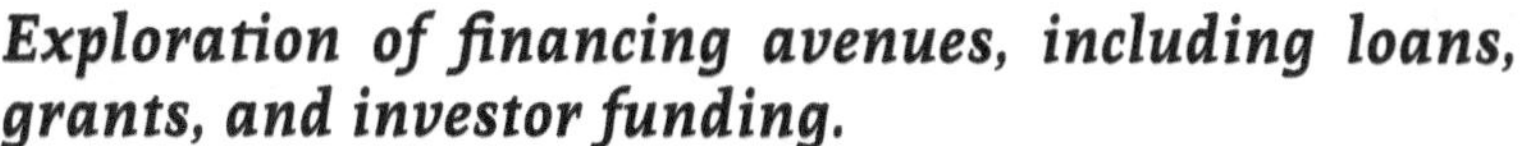

Exploration of financing avenues, including loans, grants, and investor funding.

Securing adequate financing is a pivotal step for ceramics businesses at various stages of growth, from initial setup and expansion to overcoming temporary cash flow challenges. A diverse range of financing options is available, each with its own set of advantages, requirements, and considerations.

This section will point out the primary financing avenues for ceramics businesses, including traditional loans, grants, and investor funding, providing insights into how to navigate the financing landscape effectively.

Traditional Loans

Traditional loans from banks or credit unions are a common source of funding for ceramics businesses. They can be used for a variety of purposes, such as purchasing equipment, expanding facilities, or increasing working capital. To secure a loan, businesses typically need to demonstrate a solid business plan, good credit history, and the ability to repay the loan.

Advantages:

Predictable repayment terms and interest rates.

No requirement to give up equity.

Considerations:

May require collateral.

Approval process can be lengthy and challenging for startups or businesses with poor credit.

Small Business Administration (SBA) Loans

SBA loans are partially guaranteed by the U.S. Small Business Administration, reducing the risk to lenders and often resulting in more favorable terms for the borrower. SBA loans can be an excellent option for ceramics businesses that may not qualify for traditional loans.

Advantages:

Lower down payments and competitive interest rates.

Longer repayment terms.

Considerations:

Extensive documentation and stringent qualification criteria.

The application process can be time-consuming.

Business Lines of Credit

A business line of credit offers flexible borrowing options, allowing businesses to draw funds up to a certain limit as needed. This can be particularly useful for managing cash flow fluctuations or unexpected expenses.

Advantages:

Pay interest only on the amount borrowed.

Can be reused as the balance is paid off.

Considerations:

May have higher interest rates compared to traditional loans.

Requires discipline to manage effectively and avoid overextension.

Grants

Grants are funds provided by government entities, non-profit organizations, or private foundations that do not need to be repaid. They are often awarded based on specific criteria, such as business location, industry, or the owner's background.

Advantages:

No repayment required, making them an attractive form of financing.

Can provide credibility and public relations boost.

Considerations:

Highly competitive with specific eligibility requirements.

The application process can be complex and time-consuming.

Crowdfunding

Crowdfunding platforms allow businesses to raise small amounts of money from a large number of people, typically via the internet. There are different types of crowdfunding, including rewards-based, equity-based, and debt crowdfunding.

Advantages:

Access to a broad audience of potential supporters.

Can validate the market demand for a product.

Considerations:

Success is not guaranteed and depends on effective campaign marketing.

Equity crowdfunding involves giving up a portion of business ownership.

Angel Investors and Venture Capital

Angel investors are high-net-worth individuals who provide capital for a business start-up, usually in exchange for convertible debt or ownership equity. Venture capitalists are firms that invest in high-growth potential businesses with the expectation of high returns.

Advantages:

Significant amounts of capital can be raised.

Investors often provide valuable expertise and business connections.

Considerations:

Giving up a portion of business equity.

Investors typically seek businesses with high growth potential, which may not be a fit for all ceramics businesses.

Case Study: Financing a Ceramics Studio Expansion

A ceramics studio sought to expand its production capacity and open a retail storefront. The owners explored several financing options, ultimately deciding on a combination of an SBA loan and a local government grant designed to support small businesses in the arts sector.

The SBA loan provided the bulk of the funding needed for the expansion, offering favorable terms that made the monthly payments manageable. The grant covered specific costs associated with the retail storefront setup, including renovations and initial marketing efforts. This combination of financing options allowed the studio to achieve its expansion goals without overextending its financial resources.

Strategies for Securing Financing

Prepare a Strong Business Plan: A detailed business plan is crucial when seeking financing, as it demonstrates the viability of your business and your plan for using the funds.

Understand Your Credit Score: Your personal and business credit scores can significantly impact your ability to secure financing. Understand your credit score and take steps to improve it if necessary.

Explore Multiple Options: Don't limit yourself to one type of financing. Explore various sources to find the best fit for your business needs and goals.

Leverage Industry Networks: Networking with other ceramics professionals and industry associations can provide valuable insights into financing opportunities and strategies.

Consider the Full Cost: When evaluating financing options, consider all costs involved, including interest, fees, and any equity you might be giving up.

Navigating the financing landscape can be challenging for ceramics businesses, but understanding the range of available options is the first step toward securing the necessary funding. Whether through traditional loans, grants, investor funding, or alternative financing methods, there are numerous pathways to support the growth and sustainability of your ceramics business.

By carefully assessing each option's advantages and considerations and preparing a strong case for funding, ceramics entrepreneurs can successfully secure the financial resources needed to achieve their business objectives.

ppp

Summary

"Financing Options for Ceramics Businesses" explores the diverse avenues available for securing financial support, tailored to the unique needs of the ceramics industry. This comprehensive guide covers traditional loans, which provide a direct influx of capital often necessary for equipment purchases or facility upgrades. It also delves into grants, highlighting government and private funding opportunities specifically aimed at supporting arts and crafts, including ceramics, which can offer financial assistance without the requirement of repayment. Furthermore, the guide examines investor funding options, from angel investors to venture capitalists interested in the creative and commercial potential of innovative ceramics businesses. Each financing option is discussed with its advantages, limitations, and suitability for different stages of business growth, providing ceramics entrepreneurs with the knowledge to make informed decisions on how to best finance their operations for sustainability and expansion.

ᑫᑫᑫ

FIFTEEN

RISK MANAGEMENT IN THE CERAMICS INDUSTRY

Identifying and mitigating financial risks specific to ceramics production and sales.

Risk management is an essential practice for ceramics businesses, aimed at identifying, assessing, and mitigating risks that could impact financial stability and operational efficiency. Given the unique challenges of ceramics production and sales, including the fragile nature of the products, the fluctuating costs of materials, and market demand variability, a tailored approach to risk management is necessary.

Ceramics businesses face risks at every stage of the production and sales process, from sourcing raw materials to delivering finished products to customers. Unforeseen events such as supply chain disruptions, quality control issues, and economic downturns can significantly impact profitability and competitiveness.

Therefore, proactive risk management strategies are vital to anticipate and address potential threats before they escalate into larger problems.

By implementing robust risk management processes, ceramics businesses can enhance their resilience and adaptability in an ever-changing market environment.

This involves identifying and prioritizing risks, developing mitigation plans, and regularly monitoring and reviewing risk factors to ensure proactive management.

Additionally, fostering a culture of risk awareness and accountability among employees can help create a more responsive and agile organization capable of navigating challenges effectively.

Identifying Key Financial Risks

1. Market Demand Fluctuations

The demand for ceramics can be influenced by changing consumer preferences, economic conditions, and trends in home decor. A decrease in demand can significantly affect sales revenue and profitability.

2. Cost Volatility

Ceramics businesses face volatility in the costs of raw materials (clay, glazes) and energy (especially for kiln firing), which can fluctuate due to market conditions, geopolitical events, and environmental factors.

3. Production Risks

The ceramics production process is intricate and prone to risks such as breakage, defects, and production delays. These risks can increase costs and reduce the availability of products for sale.

4. Supply Chain Disruptions

Disruptions in the supply chain, whether due to natural disasters, supplier issues, or transportation delays, can impact the availability of raw materials and finished products, affecting production schedules and sales.

5. Regulatory and Compliance Risks

Ceramics businesses must comply with various regulations, including environmental regulations related to kiln emissions and workplace safety standards. Non-compliance can result in fines, legal action, and reputational damage.

Strategies for Mitigating Financial Risks

1. Diversification of Products and Markets

Diversifying the product range and exploring new markets can reduce dependence on a single product line or customer segment, mitigating the impact of demand fluctuations. Offering a mix of functional ware, decorative pieces, and custom commissions can appeal to a broader customer base.

2. Cost Management and Efficiency Improvements

Implementing cost management strategies, such as negotiating with suppliers for better prices or investing in energy-efficient kilns, can help control production costs. Regularly reviewing and optimizing production processes for efficiency can also reduce waste and lower costs.

3. Quality Control and Process Optimization

Establishing rigorous quality control measures and continually optimizing production processes can minimize the risk of defects and breakage. Training staff in best practices and investing in reliable equipment can improve production quality and consistency.

4. Supply Chain Management

Building strong relationships with suppliers and developing a diversified supplier base can reduce the risk of supply chain disruptions. Maintaining an adequate inventory of critical raw materials and having backup suppliers can ensure continuity of production.

5. Regulatory Compliance and Environmental Management

Staying informed about relevant regulations and implementing compliance programs can mitigate the risk of regulatory violations. Adopting environmentally friendly practices, such as recycling waste materials and using non-toxic glazes, can also minimize environmental impact and comply with regulations.

6. Financial Planning and Cash Reserve Maintenance

Effective financial planning, including cash flow forecasting and budgeting, is crucial for managing financial risks. Maintaining a cash reserve can provide a buffer against unexpected expenses or downturns in sales.

7. Insurance Coverage

Appropriate insurance coverage, including property insurance, liability insurance, and business interruption insurance, can provide financial protection against various risks, including accidents, natural disasters, and theft.

Case Study: Risk Management in a Ceramics Studio

A ceramics studio specializing in bespoke dinnerware sets implemented a comprehensive risk management plan to address the financial risks specific to its operations.

Recognizing the volatility in market demand, the studio diversified its product range to include both high-end, custom pieces and a more affordable line of functional ware, broadening its customer base.

To mitigate cost volatility, the studio entered into long-term contracts with its clay and glaze suppliers, securing stable prices for essential materials. It also invested in an energy-efficient kiln, reducing energy costs and environmental impact.

Quality control was enhanced through the implementation of a detailed production checklist and regular staff training sessions, significantly reducing the rate of defects and breakage. The studio also developed a diversified supplier network to minimize supply chain disruptions, ensuring a consistent supply of raw materials.

Compliance with regulatory requirements was ensured through regular reviews of environmental and safety regulations, and the studio implemented measures to reduce kiln emissions and improve workplace safety.

Finally, the studio conducted a thorough review of its insurance coverage, ensuring adequate protection against property damage, liability claims, and business interruptions.

Implementing Effective Risk Management

Implementing effective risk management in a ceramics business involves several key steps:

Risk Assessment: Regularly identify and assess potential risks to the business, considering both internal and external factors.

Risk Prioritization: Prioritize risks based on their potential impact and likelihood, focusing on the most critical risks first.

Strategy Development: Develop strategies to mitigate identified risks, including both preventive measures and contingency plans.

Implementation and Monitoring: Implement risk management strategies and continuously monitor their effectiveness, making adjustments as necessary.

Communication and Training: Ensure that all staff are aware of potential risks and trained in risk management practices, fostering a culture of risk awareness and proactive management.

Risk management is a vital component of a successful ceramics business, enabling entrepreneurs to identify, assess, and mitigate financial risks associated with ceramics production and sales.

By implementing strategies such as product and market diversification, cost management, quality control, supply chain management, regulatory compliance, financial planning, and insurance coverage, ceramics businesses can protect themselves against financial uncertainties.

Regularly reviewing and updating the risk management plan, in light of changing market conditions and business objectives, ensures ongoing relevance and effectiveness.

Through diligent risk management, ceramics businesses can achieve financial stability, operational efficiency, and sustainable growth.

ᐅᐅᐅ

Summary

"Risk Management in the Ceramics Industry" addresses the critical need to identify and mitigate financial risks inherent in ceramics production and sales. This guide emphasizes the unique challenges faced by ceramics businesses, from the volatility of raw material prices and the potential for product breakage during production and shipping to fluctuations in market demand. It outlines strategies for managing these risks, such as diversifying product lines, implementing stringent quality control processes, and developing flexible pricing strategies. Additionally, the guide discusses the importance of insurance and hedging options to protect against significant financial losses. By adopting a proactive approach to risk management, ceramics entrepreneurs can safeguard their businesses against unforeseen financial setbacks, ensuring stability and fostering a resilient growth path in the ever-evolving ceramics market.

▷▷▷

SIXTEEN

SUSTAINABLE FINANCIAL PRACTICES

Integrating sustainability into financial practices to support long-term success in the ceramics industry.

Integrating sustainable financial practices is crucial for ceramics businesses aiming for long-term success. As consumers increasingly value sustainability, businesses in the ceramics industry must adapt their financial strategies to align with environmentally friendly and socially responsible practices.

This section will reveal how ceramics businesses can incorporate sustainability into their financial practices, covering aspects such as green financing, cost management, revenue diversification, and investment in sustainable practices.

Understanding Sustainable Financial Practices

Sustainable financial practices involve making business decisions that not only ensure economic viability but also consider environmental and social impacts. This approach seeks to balance profit with principles, ensuring that business growth does not come at the expense of the planet or people.

Green Financing

Green financing refers to funding allocated specifically for projects that have positive environmental impacts, such as energy efficiency, pollution reduction, and sustainable resource use. Ceramics businesses can explore green loans, grants, and incentives offered by governments, financial institutions, and international organizations to support eco-friendly upgrades or initiatives.

Advantages:

Access to capital for sustainability projects.

Potentially lower interest rates or financial incentives.

Strategies:

Identify green financing opportunities relevant to the ceramics industry, such as investments in energy-efficient kilns or waste recycling systems.

Prepare detailed project proposals highlighting the environmental benefits to meet the criteria for green financing.

Cost Management and Efficiency

Sustainable cost management involves identifying ways to reduce costs through eco-friendly practices. This can include reducing energy consumption, minimizing waste, and optimizing resource use, which not only lowers expenses but also reduces environmental impact.

Advantages:

Lower operating costs through energy savings and waste reduction.

Enhanced reputation among consumers who value sustainability.

Strategies:

Conduct an energy audit to identify opportunities for savings and invest in energy-efficient equipment.

Implement waste reduction programs, such as recycling clay scraps and reusing water from the production process.

Revenue Diversification through Sustainable Products

Diversifying revenue by developing and marketing sustainable ceramics products can attract environmentally conscious consumers and open up new market opportunities. This includes products made from recycled materials, designed for longevity, or produced using low-impact methods.

Advantages:

Access to niche markets and premium pricing opportunities.

Alignment with consumer trends favoring sustainability.

Strategies:

Research and develop sustainable product lines that meet the needs and *preferences of target markets.*

Leverage marketing and branding to highlight the environmental benefits of your products.

Investment in Sustainable Practices

Investing in sustainable practices involves dedicating resources to initiatives that improve the environmental and social impact of the business. This can range from adopting renewable energy sources to supporting community initiatives.

Advantages:

Long-term cost savings and risk reduction.

Improved brand loyalty and employee engagement.

Strategies:

Prioritize investments in technologies and practices that offer significant environmental benefits and align with business goals.

Measure and report on the impact of these investments to stakeholders.

Case Study: A Ceramics Studio's Journey to Sustainability

A small ceramics studio was determined to integrate sustainability into its financial practices. The studio began by securing a green loan to upgrade to an energy-efficient kiln, significantly reducing energy consumption and carbon emissions. The savings achieved from lower utility bills were reinvested into developing a new line of products made from recycled materials, appealing to a growing segment of eco-conscious consumers.

To further enhance its sustainability credentials, the studio implemented a water recycling system, reducing its water usage by 40%. The studio also became involved in local environmental initiatives, sponsoring workshops on sustainable living and supporting tree planting campaigns.

The commitment to sustainability attracted positive media attention, leading to increased brand loyalty among existing customers and attracting new ones. The studio's financial performance improved, with increased sales and reduced operating costs, demonstrating the economic viability of sustainable financial practices.

Implementing Sustainable Financial Practices

Conduct a Sustainability Audit: Assess current practices to identify areas where sustainability can be enhanced, focusing on energy use, waste management, and resource efficiency.

Set Clear Sustainability Goals: Define specific, measurable goals for integrating sustainability into financial practices, such as reducing energy consumption by a certain percentage or launching a sustainable product line.

Engage Stakeholders: Involve employees, customers, suppliers, and the local community in your sustainability efforts, encouraging feedback and participation.

Monitor Progress and Adjust Strategies: Regularly review the impact of sustainable financial practices, using metrics such as energy savings, waste reduction, and sales of sustainable products. Adjust strategies as needed to achieve sustainability goals.

Integrating sustainability into financial practices is not just an ethical choice but a strategic one that can support the long-term success of ceramics businesses. By embracing green financing, efficient cost management, sustainable product development, and investment in eco-friendly practices, ceramics businesses can reduce their environmental impact, tap into new markets, and build a strong, sustainable brand.

Implementing these practices requires commitment, creativity, and collaboration, but the benefits – for the business, the environment, and society – are substantial. As the ceramics industry continues to evolve, those businesses that prioritize sustainability will be well-positioned to thrive in the future.

Summary

"Sustainable Financial Practices" advocates for the integration of sustainability into the financial practices of ceramics businesses, highlighting its importance for long-term success in the industry. This guide emphasizes the dual focus on environmental sustainability and financial health, illustrating how eco-friendly production methods can lead to cost savings and open up new market opportunities. It explores strategies such as investing in energy-efficient kilns, recycling clay and materials, and adopting green packaging solutions. Additionally, the guide addresses the financial benefits of building a brand that is committed to sustainability, appealing to a growing demographic of environmentally conscious consumers. By implementing sustainable financial practices, ceramics businesses not only contribute to the well-being of the planet but also enhance their profitability and resilience in a competitive market, securing their success for the future.

ᐅᐅᐅ

SEVENTEEN

TECHNOLOGY AND FINANCIAL MANAGEMENT

Leveraging technology for improved financial management in ceramics businesses.

In the dynamic world of ceramics businesses, the integration of technology into financial management practices represents a strategic leverage point for enhancing efficiency, accuracy, and strategic insight.

As the industry navigates the complexities of global markets, fluctuating material costs, and evolving consumer preferences, technology offers tools to streamline operations, improve decision-making, and foster sustainable growth.

Now we will learn how ceramics businesses can harness technology to revolutionize their financial management, covering aspects from accounting systems and inventory management to analytics and forecasting.

The Role of Technology in Financial Management

Technology plays a crucial role in modern financial management, offering solutions that automate routine tasks, provide real-time financial data, and support strategic planning. For ceramics businesses, this means more time can be devoted to creative and strategic endeavors, rather than being bogged down by manual financial processes.

Accounting and Bookkeeping Software

Modern accounting software automates bookkeeping tasks, tracks financial transactions, and generates detailed financial reports. This not only ensures accuracy but also provides business owners with a clear view of their financial health.

Features to look for:

Integration with bank accounts and payment systems for real-time transaction tracking.

Customizable reporting capabilities to analyze revenue streams, cost centers, and profitability.

Benefits:

Reduces the risk of human error in financial transactions.

Saves time and resources, allowing focus on core business activities.

Inventory Management Systems

Effective inventory management is crucial for ceramics businesses, where the cost of materials and the timing of production cycles play significant roles in financial performance. Advanced inventory management systems can track stock levels, reorder materials automatically, and analyze inventory turnover rates.

Features to look for:

Real-time inventory tracking to prevent stockouts or overstocking.

Integration with suppliers for seamless ordering and restocking processes.

Benefits:

Optimizes inventory levels, reducing storage costs and minimizing waste.

Enhances production planning and efficiency, directly impacting profitability.

Financial Analytics and Forecasting Tools

Financial analytics tools extract insights from financial data, enabling ceramics businesses to identify trends, assess performance, and forecast future financial scenarios. These tools can analyze sales data, cost patterns, and market dynamics to inform strategic decision-making.

Features to look for:

Predictive analytics capabilities to forecast sales, cash flow, and market trends.

Dashboard interfaces that provide at-a-glance views of key financial indicators.

Benefits:

Supports informed strategic planning and risk management.

Identifies opportunities for cost savings, revenue enhancement, and market expansion.

Payment Processing Solutions

The adoption of modern payment processing solutions, including online payments, mobile payments, and electronic invoices, can streamline the sales process, improve cash flow, and enhance customer satisfaction.

Features to look for:

Secure payment processing to protect financial data and build customer trust.

Integration with accounting software for automatic recording and reconciliation of sales transactions.

Benefits:

Expands sales opportunities by accommodating a range of payment methods.

Reduces administrative overhead associated with payment processing and record-keeping.

Cloud Computing

Cloud computing offers ceramics businesses the flexibility to access financial management tools and data from anywhere, at any time. This enables business owners to make informed decisions on the go and facilitates collaboration among team members.

Features to look for:

Scalable storage and computing resources to match business needs.

Robust security measures to protect sensitive financial data.

Benefits:

Facilitates remote work and collaboration, increasing operational flexibility.

Ensures data is backed up and recoverable in case of hardware failure or other disasters.

Implementing Technology Solutions

Implementing new technology in financial management requires a strategic approach to ensure alignment with business goals, user needs, and operational capabilities.

Assess Needs and Objectives: Clearly define what you aim to achieve with new technology, whether it's improving efficiency, gaining financial insights, or enhancing decision-making.

Research and Select Solutions: Investigate available technologies, considering factors such as features, scalability, integration capabilities, and cost. Opt for solutions that offer the best fit for your business's unique needs.

Plan for Implementation: Develop a detailed implementation plan, including timelines, training programs for staff, and data migration strategies.

Monitor and Evaluate: After implementation, continuously monitor the performance of new technology solutions against your objectives. Be prepared to make adjustments or seek additional training as needed.

Case Study: A Ceramics Studio Embraces Financial Technology

A small ceramics studio, facing challenges with manual bookkeeping and inventory management, decided to embrace technology to streamline its financial operations. After assessing its needs, the studio implemented an integrated financial management system that combined accounting, inventory management, and sales analytics.

The new system automated daily bookkeeping tasks, provided real-time inventory visibility, and offered insights into sales trends and profitability by product line. This allowed the studio to optimize its production schedule, reduce excess inventory, and focus on high-margin products.

As a result, the studio saw a significant improvement in its financial performance, with increased efficiency leading to higher profitability and more time available for creative work.

For ceramics businesses in today's competitive market, leveraging technology in financial management is not just an option but a necessity for sustainable growth. By adopting advanced accounting systems, inventory management tools, analytics, and cloud solutions, ceramics businesses can achieve greater efficiency, insight, and strategic agility.

Implementing these technologies requires careful planning and commitment, but the rewards—improved financial control, enhanced decision-making, and the ability to focus on core creative and strategic activities—far outweigh the investment.

❧❧❧

Summary

"Technology and Financial Management" explores the transformative impact of technology on improving financial management within the ceramics industry. This guide delves into the adoption of digital tools and software solutions that streamline accounting processes, enhance inventory control, and facilitate precise cost and profit analysis. It highlights the benefits of using technology to automate routine financial tasks, allowing ceramics entrepreneurs to focus more on creative and strategic aspects of their business. Additionally, the guide examines how e-commerce platforms and online marketing can expand market reach and increase sales. By leveraging technology, ceramics businesses can achieve greater efficiency, accuracy in financial reporting, and insightful data analysis, leading to better decision-making and ultimately, stronger financial performance in a competitive landscape.

❧❧❧

EIGHTEEN

INTERNATIONAL TRADE AND FINANCE

Navigating the complexities of exporting and importing ceramics, including currency exchange and international payments.

The international trade of ceramics embodies a world of art, culture, and commerce. From the finest porcelain to robust earthenware, ceramics traverse the globe, enriching lives and spaces. However, the journey of ceramics from the kiln to international markets is paved with complex challenges, particularly in the realms of currency exchange and international payments.

This chapter aims to unravel these intricacies, offering guidance to navigate the global landscape of exporting and importing ceramics.

Understanding the Ceramics Market

The global ceramics market is diverse, with each region specializing in unique styles and materials. Exporters and importers must have a keen understanding of market demands, regulatory compliance, and quality standards.

Moreover, understanding the nuances of cultural significance can provide a competitive edge in global markets.

Navigating Currency Exchange in International Ceramics Trade

Currency exchange rates fluctuate, impacting the cost and revenue of international transactions. For exporters and importers of ceramics, managing currency risk is crucial to maintaining profitability.

Forward Contracts: Lock in exchange rates for future transactions, providing cost certainty and protecting against adverse currency movements.

Options Contracts: Offer flexibility, allowing traders to benefit from favorable currency movements while providing protection against unfavorable changes.

Multi-Currency Accounts: Enable businesses to hold, receive, and pay in multiple currencies, reducing the need for constant currency conversion and mitigating exchange rate risk.

International Payments and Financing

Efficiently managing international payments is pivotal for the seamless trade of ceramics. The choice of payment method influences risk, cash flow, and relationships between buyers and sellers.

Letters of Credit (LCs): LCs provide a guarantee from the buyer's bank, ensuring payment to the seller upon fulfilling the terms of the contract. While offering security, LCs can be complex and expensive.

Open Account Transactions: Allow payment after the goods are delivered, favoring the buyer but increasing risk for the seller. Export credit insurance can mitigate this risk, protecting sellers against non-payment.

Wire Transfers: Offer a quick and secure method for international payments. However, transaction fees and exchange rate margins can add costs.

Trade Financing Solutions

Trade financing plays a critical role in supporting the ceramics industry, offering solutions to bridge the gap between shipment and payment.

Export Financing: Governments and financial institutions provide loans and insurance products to exporters, reducing the financial strain and risks of international trade.

Factoring and Forfaiting: Selling receivables at a discount (factoring) or using forfaiting to eliminate payment risks by selling the importer's payment obligations at a discount can provide immediate cash flow and risk mitigation.

Mitigating Risks in Ceramics Trade

International trade involves various risks, from currency fluctuations to non-payment and political instability. Exporters and importers must adopt comprehensive risk management strategies.

Currency Hedging: Protect against currency risk through financial instruments like futures, options, and forwards.

Quality Control and Compliance: Implement stringent quality control measures and comply with international standards to avoid disputes and ensure customer satisfaction.

Political and Credit Risk Insurance: Insure against non-payment, confiscation, expropriation, and political unrest, securing the financial interests of businesses involved in the ceramics trade.

Technological Advancements in Trade Finance

Technology is revolutionizing international trade finance, making transactions more secure, efficient, and transparent.

Blockchain: Offers a secure and transparent way to document transactions, reducing fraud and speeding up the documentation process.

Digital Platforms for Trade Finance: Provide streamlined access to financing options, allowing businesses to quickly secure the funds needed for international trade.

Exporting and importing ceramics on the international stage involves navigating a complex array of financial and regulatory challenges. By understanding and effectively managing currency exchange and international payments, businesses can mitigate risks and capitalize on global opportunities.

The fusion of traditional trade practices with innovative financial solutions and technology paves the way for a flourishing global ceramics market.

As we move forward, the key to success lies in adaptability, strategic planning, and a deep understanding of the intricate dance of international trade and finance.

❧❧❧

Summary

"International Trade and Finance" delves into the complexities of exporting and importing ceramics, focusing on the critical aspects of currency exchange and international payments. This summary highlights the challenges ceramics businesses face in the global market, such as fluctuating currency values that can significantly impact costs and profits. It outlines strategies for managing these financial risks, including the use of forward contracts to lock in exchange rates and the benefits of opening multi-currency accounts for easier transactions. The guide also explores various international payment methods, such as letters of credit and wire transfers, providing ceramics entrepreneurs with the knowledge to choose the best options for their business needs. By navigating these complexities with informed strategies, ceramics businesses can expand their global footprint while minimizing financial risks associated with international trade.

᭧᭧᭧

NINETEEN

Legal Considerations and Financial Compliance

Legal issues affecting the ceramics industry and ensuring compliance with financial regulations.

Navigating the legal landscape and ensuring compliance with financial regulations are crucial aspects of managing a ceramics business. The ceramics industry, like any other, is subject to a variety of legal considerations ranging from intellectual property rights to environmental regulations, each with implications for financial management and operational sustainability.

Let's light on the key legal issues affecting the ceramics industry and outlines strategies for ensuring compliance with financial regulations, thereby safeguarding the business's reputation and financial health.

Intellectual Property Rights

Intellectual property (IP) rights are of paramount importance in the ceramics industry, where unique designs and artistic works are the lifeblood of many businesses. Protecting these assets is essential for maintaining competitive advantage and securing revenue streams.

Key Considerations:

Copyrights: Automatically protect artistic works, including ceramics designs, from the moment of creation. Ensuring that copyright notices are clearly displayed on products and marketing materials can deter infringement.

Trademarks: Protect brand names, logos, and slogans that distinguish a business's products. Registering trademarks can prevent competitors from using similar marks that could confuse customers.

Patents: While less common in the ceramics industry, patents can protect innovative manufacturing processes or novel materials. Obtaining a patent grants exclusive rights to use the invention, providing a competitive edge.

Strategies for Compliance:

Conduct regular IP audits to identify assets that require protection.

Register trademarks and patents where applicable and enforce rights against infringers.

Include IP clauses in contracts with employees, contractors, and business partners to clarify ownership of creations.

Environmental Regulations

The ceramics industry involves processes that can have significant environmental impacts, including kiln emissions and waste generation. Compliance with environmental regulations is not only a legal requirement but also a factor increasingly considered by consumers when making purchasing decisions.

Key Considerations:

Emissions: Kilns, especially those fired by fossil fuels, emit pollutants that may be regulated under local or national environmental laws.

Waste Management: Proper disposal of hazardous materials, such as certain glazes containing heavy metals, is regulated to prevent environmental contamination.

Resource Use: Regulations may also cover the extraction and use of raw materials, aiming to ensure sustainable sourcing practices.

Strategies for Compliance:

Invest in energy-efficient and lower-emission kilns to reduce environmental impact and comply with emissions standards.

Implement waste reduction and recycling programs to minimize hazardous waste and ensure proper disposal.

Source raw materials ethically and sustainably, considering both environmental impact and compliance with legal standards.

Employment Laws

As ceramics businesses grow and hire employees, compliance with employment laws becomes increasingly important. These laws cover a wide range of issues from wages and working hours to workplace safety and discrimination.

Key Considerations:

Wages and Benefits: Ensuring employees are paid at least the minimum wage and are provided any mandated benefits.

Workplace Safety: Compliance with occupational safety and health regulations, particularly relevant in ceramics studios where there are risks associated with equipment and materials.

Equal Employment Opportunity: Adherence to laws prohibiting discrimination in hiring and employment practices.

Strategies for Compliance:

Regularly review employment practices and policies to ensure they meet legal requirements.

Provide training to employees and managers on workplace safety and discrimination laws.

Keep accurate records of employment terms, wages, and incident reports to demonstrate compliance in the event of an audit or legal challenge.

Tax Compliance

Compliance with tax laws is critical for ceramics businesses to avoid penalties and maintain good standing with tax authorities. This includes accurate reporting of income, timely payment of taxes, and adherence to tax regulations related to sales, payroll, and imports/exports.

Key Considerations:

Income Tax: Proper reporting of business income and expenses to calculate taxable income accurately.

Sales Tax: Collection and remittance of sales tax on goods sold, which may vary by location.

Payroll Tax: Withholding and payment of payroll taxes for employees, including income tax, social security, and Medicare contributions.

Strategies for Compliance:

Utilize accounting software to track financial transactions accurately and generate reports required for tax filings.

Stay informed about changes in tax laws that may affect the business, including rates, filing requirements, and deductions.

Consult with tax professionals to ensure compliance, especially when dealing with complex issues or international sales.

Consumer Protection Laws

Consumer protection laws aim to ensure that products are safe for use and that businesses do not engage in deceptive practices. Compliance with these laws is essential for building trust with customers and avoiding legal repercussions.

Key Considerations:

Product Safety: Ceramics used for food and drink must meet safety standards regarding lead and cadmium levels.

Marketing and Sales Practices: Adherence to laws governing advertising, online sales, and customer privacy.

Strategies for Compliance:

Implement quality control processes to ensure products meet safety standards.

Review marketing materials and sales practices to ensure they are truthful and do not mislead customers.

Protect customer data in accordance with privacy laws, especially for online sales.

Navigating Legal Challenges

Despite best efforts to comply with all relevant laws, ceramics businesses may occasionally face legal challenges. Being prepared to address these challenges is crucial for minimizing their impact.

Strategies for Mitigation:

Establish a relationship with a legal advisor experienced in the ceramics industry or small business law to provide guidance when issues arise.

Develop a contingency plan for legal challenges, including budgeting for potential legal expenses.

Engage in mediation or alternative dispute resolution methods where possible to resolve conflicts without litigation.

Legal considerations and financial compliance are integral to the successful operation of a ceramics business. By understanding and adhering to intellectual property rights, environmental regulations, employment laws, tax compliance, and consumer protection laws, ceramics businesses can mitigate risks and build a solid foundation for long-term success.

Implementing strategies for compliance, staying informed about legal changes, and seeking professional advice when necessary are key steps in navigating the complex legal landscape of the ceramics industry.

❦❦❦

Summary

"Legal Considerations and Financial Compliance" addresses the critical legal issues affecting the ceramics industry and the importance of ensuring compliance with financial regulations. This guide offers a comprehensive overview of the regulatory landscape, including copyright laws relevant to ceramic designs, import/export restrictions, and safety standards for materials and production processes. It emphasizes the necessity for ceramics businesses to stay informed about tax laws and financial reporting requirements to avoid penalties and legal complications. The guide provides practical advice on establishing internal policies and procedures to maintain compliance and protect intellectual property. By prioritizing legal considerations and financial compliance, ceramics entrepreneurs can safeguard their operations against legal challenges, ensuring a stable and prosperous business environment.

▷▷▷

TWENTY

Case Studies of Successful Ceramics Businesses

❦

Real-world examples of ceramics businesses that have achieved financial success.

Exploring the pathways to success through real-world examples provides invaluable insights for aspiring and established ceramics businesses alike. Following brief case studies of ceramics businesses that have carved out a niche for themselves, showcasing the diverse strategies they employed to achieve financial success.

These examples highlight the importance of innovative design, strategic marketing, operational efficiency, and adaptability in navigating the challenges and opportunities of the ceramics industry.

Case Study 1: Eco-Friendly Innovations

Background: GreenPottery, a startup founded by two environmental enthusiasts, focused on creating eco-friendly and sustainable ceramic products. Their unique selling proposition was their use of recycled materials and environmentally friendly production processes.

Strategies for Success:

Innovation in Materials: GreenPottery developed a proprietary blend of recycled clay and organic materials, reducing the environmental impact of their products.

Sustainability Certification: They obtained certification from several environmental organizations, enhancing their brand image and appealing to eco-conscious consumers.

Targeted Marketing: The company leveraged social media and eco-friendly blogs to market their products, emphasizing their sustainability and unique design elements.

Outcome: GreenPottery's commitment to sustainability and innovative product design helped them carve out a niche market. Their products were featured in several eco-friendly lifestyle magazines, leading to a surge in online sales. They expanded their product line to include home decor items, further increasing their revenue streams.

Case Study 2: Embracing Digital Transformation

Background: CeramixArt, a traditional ceramics studio with a history spanning over three decades, faced declining sales as consumer buying behaviors shifted online. The second-generation owner decided to embrace digital transformation to revitalize the business.

Strategies for Success:

E-commerce Platform: CeramixArt launched an online store, offering their traditional ceramics alongside new, modern designs to attract a broader customer base.

Digital Marketing: They invested in digital marketing, including SEO and social media advertising, to drive traffic to their online store.

Customer Engagement: By implementing a customer relationship management (CRM) system, CeramixArt personalized their marketing efforts and improved customer service, leading to higher customer retention rates.

Outcome: The digital transformation strategy paid off, with online sales quickly surpassing traditional retail sales. CeramixArt also developed a strong online community of ceramics enthusiasts, further boosting their brand and customer loyalty. The business successfully transitioned into a modern, digitally savvy enterprise without losing its traditional roots.

Case Study 3: Expanding into New Markets

Background: GlobalPottery, a well-established ceramics manufacturer known for its decorative pieces, sought to expand its market presence internationally. Despite facing initial challenges with logistics and market entry, they persisted in their global expansion efforts.

Strategies for Success:

Market Research: Conducted extensive research to identify markets with high demand for decorative ceramics and understand local consumer preferences.

Strategic Partnerships: Formed partnerships with local distributors and retailers in target markets to facilitate market entry and distribution.

Product Localization: Adapted their product designs to suit local tastes and cultural preferences, increasing their appeal in new markets.

Outcome: GlobalPottery's strategic approach to international expansion significantly broadened their market reach. By adapting their products to meet local demands and leveraging strong partnerships, they established a strong presence in several key international markets, diversifying their revenue and reducing dependency on domestic sales.

Case Study 4: Leveraging Artisanal Heritage

Background: HeritageCeramics, a family-owned business specializing in artisanal pottery, leveraged its rich heritage and craftsmanship to build a premium brand. Despite competition from mass-produced ceramics, they focused on the quality and uniqueness of their handcrafted pieces.

Strategies for Success:

Brand Storytelling: Utilized their history and artisanal processes as key elements of their branding, telling their story through their website, social media, and packaging.

Collaborations and Limited Editions: Collaborated with well-known designers and artists to create limited edition pieces, generating buzz and attracting collectors.

Premium Pricing Strategy: Adopted a premium pricing strategy that reflected the craftsmanship, quality, and heritage of their products.

Outcome: HeritageCeramics' focus on their artisanal heritage and unique brand story resonated with consumers looking for authentic, handcrafted pottery. Their collaborations and limited edition pieces became highly sought after, allowing them to command premium prices and achieve significant financial success.

Case Study 5: Streamlining Operations for Efficiency

Background: EfficientClay, a ceramics production company, faced challenges with production inefficiencies and rising costs. By focusing on operational efficiency and cost management, they aimed to improve their profit margins without compromising product quality.

Strategies for Success:

Process Optimization: Analyzed and optimized every step of the production process to eliminate waste and reduce production time.

Technology Investment: Invested in new kilns and automation technologies to enhance production efficiency and energy use.

Supply Chain Management: Negotiated better terms with suppliers and implemented just-in-time inventory management to reduce material costs and minimize storage expenses.

Outcome: The focus on streamlining operations resulted in significant cost savings and increased production capacity.

EfficientClay was able to reduce its production costs by 20% while maintaining high product quality, leading to improved profitability and competitive pricing.

These case studies of successful ceramics businesses highlight the diversity of strategies that can lead to financial success in the ceramics industry. Whether through embracing sustainability, digital transformation, market expansion, leveraging artisanal heritage, or optimizing operations, these businesses demonstrate the importance of innovation, strategic planning, and adaptability. By understanding and applying the lessons from these real-world examples, ceramics businesses can navigate the challenges of the industry and carve out their path to financial success.

ᗡᗡᗡ

Summary

"Case Studies of Successful Ceramics Businesses" presents real-world examples of ceramics businesses that have navigated the path to financial success, offering valuable insights and inspiration. This compilation showcases a variety of business models, from small artisan studios to large-scale manufacturers, highlighting the diverse strategies employed to achieve profitability. Key themes include the effective management of production costs, innovative pricing strategies, and the adoption of technology for marketing and operational efficiency. Each case study delves into the challenges faced by these businesses and the solutions implemented to overcome them, emphasizing the importance of adaptability, market research, and customer engagement. Through these success stories, ceramics entrepreneurs can learn practical lessons on financial management, strategic planning, and sustainable growth, providing a roadmap to success in the competitive ceramics industry.

▷▷▷

TWENTY-ONE

FUTURE TRENDS IN CERAMICS FINANCE

Summarizing key takeaways and looking ahead to future financial trends and challenges in the ceramics industry.

The financial foundations of ceramics encompass a multifaceted landscape that requires careful navigation and strategic planning. Throughout this book, we have explored various aspects of financial management in the ceramics industry, from costing and pricing to legal compliance and sustainability.

Drawing upon case studies and real-world examples, we have gleaned valuable insights into the strategies employed by successful ceramics businesses to achieve financial success. As we conclude our exploration, it is essential to reflect on key takeaways and consider future trends and challenges that may shape the financial landscape of the ceramics industry.

Key Takeaways

Understanding Cost Structures: A thorough understanding of cost structures in ceramics production, including both fixed and variable costs, is essential for accurate pricing and profitability analysis.

Strategic Pricing: Implementing effective pricing strategies tailored to the ceramics industry, such as value-based pricing and competition-based pricing, can enhance competitiveness and profitability.

Market Analysis and Customer Insights: Conducting comprehensive market analysis and understanding customer preferences are critical for informed decision-making and product development.

Compliance and Risk Management: Ensuring compliance with legal regulations and managing financial risks, such as those related to environmental regulations and taxation, are fundamental for long-term sustainability.

Innovation and Adaptability: Embracing innovation, whether through sustainable practices, digital transformation, or product diversification, is essential for staying competitive in an evolving market.

Operational Efficiency: Streamlining operations and optimizing processes can lead to cost savings, improved productivity, and enhanced profitability.

Strategic Partnerships and Market Expansion: Forming strategic partnerships and exploring new markets, both domestically and internationally, can facilitate business growth and revenue diversification.

Future Trends and Challenges

Looking ahead, several trends and challenges are likely to shape the financial landscape of the ceramics industry:

Sustainability Imperative: As environmental concerns continue to gain prominence, ceramics businesses will face increasing pressure to adopt sustainable practices throughout their operations, from raw material sourcing to waste management.

Digital Transformation: The adoption of digital technologies, including e-commerce platforms, digital marketing, and data analytics, will continue to reshape the ceramics industry, offering new opportunities for market reach and customer engagement.

Globalization and Market Dynamics: The globalization of markets and evolving consumer preferences will present both opportunities and challenges for ceramics businesses, requiring adaptability and strategic market positioning.

Supply Chain Resilience: Ensuring resilience and agility in the supply chain will be crucial, particularly in light of disruptions caused by factors such as natural disasters, geopolitical tensions, and global health crises.

Regulatory Changes: Ongoing changes in regulatory landscapes, including environmental regulations, taxation policies, and trade agreements, will necessitate proactive compliance measures and strategic planning.

Technological Advancements: Continued advancements in materials science and manufacturing technologies, such as 3D printing and advanced ceramics, may revolutionize the ceramics industry, offering new possibilities for product innovation and customization.

Changing Consumer Trends: Shifts in consumer preferences, including increased demand for personalized and artisanal products, will require ceramics businesses to stay attuned to market trends and adapt their offerings accordingly.

In conclusion, the ceramics industry presents a rich tapestry of opportunities and challenges in the realm of financial management. By embracing best practices in costing, pricing, compliance, and sustainability, ceramics businesses can build robust financial foundations that support long-term growth and resilience. As we look to the future, staying agile, innovative, and responsive to market dynamics will be key to navigating the evolving landscape of the ceramics industry.

By leveraging emerging trends and addressing challenges proactively, ceramics businesses can continue to thrive and flourish in the years to come, shaping the financial landscape of the industry for generations to come.

ᗺᗺᗺ

Summary

"*Future Trends in Ceramics Finance*" *summarizes key financial insights and projects forward to anticipate future trends and challenges in the ceramics industry. This summary highlights the ongoing evolution of market demands, the increasing importance of sustainability, and the role of technology in shaping financial practices. As consumer preferences continue to shift towards eco-friendly and artisanal products, ceramics businesses are expected to adapt by integrating green practices into their operations, potentially opening new market opportunities and funding avenues. Technological advancements, such as digital marketing and e-commerce platforms, are poised to play a pivotal role in reaching global audiences and streamlining financial management. Additionally, the guide anticipates challenges related to international trade, including currency fluctuations and trade regulations, urging businesses to stay agile and informed. By understanding these future trends, ceramics entrepreneurs can strategically position themselves to capitalize on opportunities, navigate potential hurdles, and drive long-term financial success in an ever-changing industry landscape.*

ᐅᐅᐅ

ᐅᐅᐅ

Citation And Reference

This book has been written after extensive research and analysis, which involved referencing various books, as well as the author's study and business experiences. The author has also searched various websites to gather valuable information and data about Financial Foundations of Ceramics: Costing, Pricing, and Profitability"

The author has taken great care to ensure that all information presented is accurate and properly cited to give credit to the sources. However, despite our best efforts, human errors may still occur. If any reader discovers any errors in this book, the author respectfully welcomes their feedback and encourages them to bring it to our attention.

Such feedback is valuable, and the author will take all necessary steps to correct any errors and improve the content of this book in future editions. Thank you for your understanding and support in this regard.

The author respects the right to freedom of speech and expression guaranteed by Article 19(1)(a) of the Constitution of India."

ϸϸϸ

Contact

Dr. Ghanshyam Trivedi
Vidres India Ceramics Pvt Ltd;
203/206, Sarthik Square, B/S Pizza Hut,
S G Road, AHMEDABAD, Gujarat-380054, India
Mobile No : +919898835000
E-Mail: tgg300@gmail.com
ghanshyamindiag20@yahoo.com

ᗠᗠᗠ

|| LOKAHA SAMASTHAHA SUKHINO BHAVANTU ||

• 175 •

www.ingramcontent.com/pod-product-compliance
Lightning Source LLC
Chambersburg PA
CBHW021441150726
47989CB00001B/335